Angelic Karma

A journey into Angels, Karma, Soul Mates & Twin Flames

Lianne Lockyer

AuthorHouse™ UK Ltd.
500 Avebury Boulevard
Central Milton Keynes, MK9 2BE
www.authorhouse.co.uk
Phone: 08001974150

© *2009 Lianne Lockyer. All rights reserved.*

No part of this book may be reproduced, stored in a retrieval system, or transmitted by any means without the written permission of the author.

First published by AuthorHouse   5/12/2009

ISBN: 978-1-4389-6555-0 (sc)

This book is printed on acid-free paper.

*This Book is dedicated to
My Husband Darran Lockyer
And my children
Shane, Stacie, Emily, Alexandria and Harriet*

~ Contents ~

Acknowledgments 5
About The Author 7
Introduction 9

Book One

Chapter 1 *Angels* 15
  The Angel Hierarchy 16
  So what is the Purpose of Angels 19
  Who and what are Angels? 23
  Ascended Masters, Elementals and Fairies 24

Chapter 2 *Walking With Angels* 29
  Angel communication 29
  Symbols and Dreams **33**
  Opening up to Angels 38
  Asking the Angels for help 40
  Angel Healing 45
  Guardian Angels 47
  Angel cards 49
  Creating Alters or Sacred Spaces 52
  Other Angel info! 56

Chapter 3 *Walking with Archangels* 58
  The Fallen Angels 58
  What are Archangels 62
  Archangel Sandalphon 64
  Archangel Jophiel 65
  Archangel Uriel 66
  Archangel Raphael 68
  Archangel Chamuel 69
  Archangel Gabriel 70
  Archangel Michael 71
  Archangel Zadkiel 73

Book 2

Chapter 4 *Karma & Reincarnation* *77*
What is Karma & Reincarnation? 77
How to Balance negative Karma 81
The Silver Violet Flame 85
Karmic Relationships 87
Karmic Marriage 90
Past Lives 91
Soul Groups 93
Parents and children 95

Chapter 5 *Soul Mates & Twin Flames* *98*
What are Twin Flames 98
The separation of twin flames 100
How do you recognise your twin flame? 101
Contact of Twin Flames 103
What is a Soul Mate ? 104
How do you recognise your Soul Mate? 106

Chapter 6 *Exercises* *108*
Protecting Yourself 108
A Walk with your Angel 111
Ascension and healing 112
Cleansing the Aura 114
Dolphin Meditation 115
Meet your Spirit Guide visualisation 116
A Healing Meditation with Archangel Raphael 118

Acknowledgments

ANGELIC KARMA

This book is written in honour of my Children,
Shane, Staci, Emily, Lou and Harriet,
to hopefully show them that you can achieve
anything that you put your mind to!
I am very proud of all of you
Also a Special Thank you to my Husband Darran,
<u>my Twin Flame</u> who was and still is, my driving
force behind the whole idea of this book,
Thank you for having faith in me and pushing
me when things got tough Xxx

About The Author

Angel Practitioner Lianne Lockyer has been working with Angels and other celestial beings for most of her life, she is a Spiritual Healer of approximately 78 different forms, is a qualified Hypnotherapist and has performed Hundreds of Past Life Regressions, and Lianne has independently studied Karma and Karmic relationships for the past ten years.

Lianne is a successful Adult Education Teacher who runs workshops and courses in developing spiritual awareness and Angelic connections. She can also be seen treading the boards in venues around the country delivering messages from spirit to amazed audiences, as well as this she and her team find time to lead on many Ghost hunts and Spirit Clearances

Lianne successfully runs her teaching academy's MYSTICALS alongside "The Lianne Lockyer National School of Mediumship and Healing" with her husband Darran Lockyer in the North West of England.

www.mystical-entertainments.com
lianne@mystical-entertainments.com

Lianne Lockyer H.P.A.I B.A.Hyp

Introduction

I wrote this book with the soul purpose of introducing to you, the absolute joy of being able to walk with your Angels, and to help you to communicate, recognise, and then of course, to work with them to improve your Life, to heal yourself, to connect to your souls' purpose and so to change your life so you can be all that you really are and to lead a rich, full and happy fulfilling life. I am also brave enough to say, that most of us, me included, have spent the majority of our lives searching for our Soul mate or Twin Flame, and are only truly happy and complete when we have rejoined them here in our present life, Unfortunately, only a few of us are lucky enough to either recognise or find the "other half of ourselves "and so with this in mind, I will try, in this book to show you how to do just that, to recognise, find, and rejoin with your soul mate & Twin Flame, by working with your Angels, after all they are here to help us, and it works! – I am living proof! I spent over 35 years without my Twin Flame, and I got to the point that I thought that maybe I was the one person that didn't have one! Or that I had missed him, then I started listening hard to what my Angels were teaching me, and then, there he was, my perfect, ideal mate, sounds sickly doesn't it! But it is true. And so now I want to share the methods with you so you to can find the joy and happiness that really is out there for you

There are numerous Angel and Archangel Books on the market today, but I have often found that a lot of these can, at best, be difficult to follow and understand especially if you are new to this walk of life.

And at worst they can be quite contradictory. Now I know there are some great, helpful books out there also, and I hope this will be one of them, I have written this book with the curious, the beginner and the more advanced in mind. I have left out many of the "technical" terms and instead written in a way that everyone should understand.

You will find that this book is in two halves, just like the twin flames, where one half would not be complete without the other half and both halves compliment the other, this book is no different. the first half (book one) is all about teaching you about the angelic Kingdom, and introducing you to the wonderful world of your angels, as well as to show you how best to work with them, then when you have mastered that you move on to the second half (book two), where you learn to join the two, and put into practice what you have learnt in order to move towards fulfilment and take the first steps towards meeting up with soul mates , putting right and understanding Karmic relationships, and then if your lucky, to recognise and rejoin your twin flame in this lifetime!

The book will finish off with some visualisations and meditations and a few exercises to practice with your angels.

I have been working with my Angels for most of my life, I am a working Medium and Angel teacher and it is through one of these classes that the idea was given to me to write this book, one of my students pointed out that almost all of the books that he had come across, he had found really hard going, and suggested that I put my courses into book format and release it, I laughed at the time, but then decided to do some research and found that he was right, the books available were quite difficult for most to understand unless you had some prior knowledge, and so Karmic Angels was born!

This book consists of background knowledge and various exercises that have helped both myself and many of my students past and present and I am sure future, from the Lianne Lockyer National school of Mediumship and Healing and Mysticals. To find our true spiritual path and our life's purpose. It is a journey into not only you but into the wonderful world of Angels. It has proved so very successful for me, my friends and my students, that I now wish to reach out to you, in order to offer you this amazing gift. Of working with your Angels

So now, relax, grab a cuppa and enjoy the journey into you

~ Book One ~

Chapter 1
Angels

Angels in History

If you have read the bible then you will know that it refers to many different types of angels, each with various duties which include - guides, protectors, messengers and angels of the Lord, the bible also mentions Cherubim, Seraphim, and Archangels, which we will go into in more detail later on, but the above three are all on the Angelic Hierarchy platform and can help us in many different ways. However when you look into the meanings of angels, their appearance and purposes you will find that they will vary hugely, dependant on history.

Artists have given us their visions of angels as winged creatures, usually beautiful figures that are glowing, shining, floating, in human form or simply as a voice. And Saints as well as everyday people will tell about being visited by or helped by angels.

Throughout history and throughout different religions and cultures Angels have been thought of as creations of a separate order from human beings, and also as the spirits of highly evolved humans. Angel scholar, Geddes McGregor, tells us the English word angel is a transcription of the Greek word "angelos". In Hebrew, angels are called "mal'ak" meaning messenger. "Mal'ak" originally meant shadow side of God. The Hebrews thought of angels as emanations of Yahweh, part of the same divine spirit. In the Christian church, angels were not believed to be emanations of God, but spirits created by God at the time He created the material world. Muhammad said angels were sent by God to seek out those places where men and women honour the deity. The angels then report back to heaven what they have heard.

Socrates tells us that Eros (a known angel figure) is a spirit who carries messages back and forth between men and gods. Another angel-like figure from mythology is Hermes, the winged messenger. With her great wings which served as a model for later depictions of angels. We can also find similar beliefs in supernatural beings in the vision of the Shaman. The Shaman takes a bird form, travels in search of the soul of his patient. Primitive cultures generally thought that illness was caused by loss of soul of some kind. There have always been people employed to go and find the soul, whether its contemporary psychologists or ancient healers.

In the middle ages, St. Augustine described the nature of an angel by relating it to an angel's purpose. " *The angels are spirits, but it is not because they are spirits that they are angels. They become angels when they are sent. The name angel refers to their office not to their nature. You ask the name of this nature, it is spirit. You ask its office, it is that of angel. In as far as he exists, an angel is a spirit, and as far as he acts he is an angel - St. Augustine.*"

The Angel Hierarchy

In Roman times is has been said that a Priest sorted the angels into a hierarchy of 9 and that has since been the commonly held belief. Heavenly counsellors and closest to God, - Seraphim, Cherubim, Thrones,
Heavenly Governors – Dominions, Virtues, Powers
Heavenly messengers – Principalities, Archangels, Angels.

I personally need more convincing that there is a Hierarchy, as we would know it. This feels like a human invention to me, especially as some of the major Archangels are also known to be on other levels such as Archangel Uriel, Angel of the North and one of the four major archangels charged with protecting the universe, who is also a Throne. Maybe it is 'as on earth so it is in heaven'

In the Kabalah there are ten Hierarchy levels, their names are Foundation, Splendour, Eternity, Beauty, Power, Grace, Knowledge, Wisdom, Understanding and Perfection. This is often portrayed as a tree. At the root stands Sandalphon, who extends through the tree into the universe. Other Angels appearing on the tree are Saphkiel, angel of contemplation, Gabriel, Michael, Raphael, Uriel and Metatron plus three others who vary according to what you are reading. We will be learning about all these angels later Below is a brief description of the various Angelic levels that are commonly accepted as decreed by the priest in Roman times.

Seraphim's - The guardians before God's throne, referred to as "the fiery spirits", they are usually pictured with six wings and flames. They constantly sing God's praise and regulate heaven. They are coloured a flaming red and gold to symbolize fire. God's grace flows through the seraphim to the Angels below, dispelling darkness and purifying the universe. It was from this order that Satan emerged. Before his fall from Grace, he was considered the Angel who outshone all others. Seraphim's are the highest order of Angels

Cherubim's- Gods record keepers and guardians of God's glory. Over the years Cherubim's have undergone radical transformations from the Assyrian leonine-monster guardian to the winged creature of the Old Testament to a chubby baby with blue wings which appeared in the 1600s. Originally, Cherubim's were depicted with multi-eyed peacock's feathers to symbolize their all-knowing character. The first Angels mentioned in the bible, God placed the Cherubim at the east of the Garden of Eden to guard the way to the Tree of Life. They are the charioteers of God and bearers of his throne.

Thrones - Referred to as "the many eyed ones", portrayed as winged wheels within wheels, whose rims were covered in eyes. They support the Throne of God and consider how God's decisions should be manifested. Their mission is to bring judgment for individual karma and society as a whole.

Dominions- These are the Angels who bring you the teachings of intuition. Through them the majesty of God is manifested. They carry sceptre and sword to symbolize the given power over all creation and decide what needs to be done to accomplish God's needs and regulate the duties of Angels to ensure the universe keeps working as it should. They appear in human shape, wearing a triple crown to signify their position over the physical form. They can be seen carrying a sceptre, holding a cross and/or a sword to symbolize the balance between the active and passive forces.

Virtues - Drawing on God's force to work miracles on earth, the "brilliant" or "shining ones" are the Angels of miracles, encouragement and blessings. Virtues are the ones who become involved whenever people are struggling with their faith. They have four blue feathered wings and war sparkling armour. They can often be seen with a sceptre, axe spear, sword and/or a shield for protection. But each of these "tools" is decorated with instruments of passion. They work hand-in-hand with the Thrones to bestow grace and rewards on those who have overcome deeds in their physical lives.

Powers- First order of Angels created by God, it is the job of the Powers to prevent the fallen Angels from taking over the world and keep the universe in balance. They also bring the power of intellect in such matters as math, geometry, astronomy and so on, making them the professors and educators.

Principalities- The protectors of religions, guardian Angels of cities, nations, rulers. They keep watch over nations and attempt to inspire their leaders to make wise decisions. Often depicted wearing soldier's garb and sandals, they are seen in human form. They provide strength to the tribes of Earth to pursue and endure their faith.

Archangels- The "chief-Angels", they carry God's messages to humans and command God's armies of Angels in constant battle with the "Sons of Darkness". They look after the affairs of humankind and act as guardian Angels to leaders of world movements. These are the Angels who stand around God's throne, ready to carry out the divine and most important decrees to humans. According to the book of Revelation, there are seven Archangels who stand in the presence of God, but only four are mentioned in the Old Testament, Michael, Gabriel, Raphael and Uriel. The identity of the other three is subject to debate. The three recognized in the Judeo-Christian belief are Raguel, Jophiel and Chamuel. Other possible candidates are Ariel, Azrael, Camael, Haniel, Jeremiel, Metatron, Raziel, Sandalphon and Zadkiel.

Angels-Celestial beings closest to humans, Angels are the intermediaries between God and mortals. Assigned by God to every human being at the time of his or her birth, they assist every aspect of life in the universe. They deal with the aspects of everyday life and act as the direct gateway for information, knowledge and communications between human kind and the God force. These Angels are seen with human bodies, wings and clothed in various garments depending on the traditions and visual acceptance of the human they have "been assigned to". In reality, Angels do not have human bodies, wings or clothing; they are made up of energy and love. The only thing Angels do not help humans do is destroy themselves, the planet and other human beings, they are always a force for all that is positive, good and true

So what is the Purpose of Angels

Over the centuries there have been many interpretations of what angels are. Here I am going to attempt to give you an insight of what they are and their purpose.
The dictionary defines Angels as" a spiritual being believed to act as an attendant or messenger of God, conventionally represented as being of human form with wings and possessing great kindness and virtue."
I believe that in the spiritual world there are realms. These realms consist of 5 main forces which control the universal or Karmic laws, they are.

1. The Spirit World:

When we pass over we pass into the spirit world or astral plane. We go through a period of finding out where we went wrong in our life or how well we handled tests given to us. So it goes without saying, that when, as living beings, we communicate with the spirit realm that these beings are not fully enlightened as yet, as they are still adjusting, and learning from the choices that they made in life. So you need to be aware that they could be confused and their knowledge is limited to their own families or events. They are allowed to give us certain information as long as they have permission from the angels and it doesn't interfere with our destiny or tests. If they try to divulge too much information the angels will sever their communication straight away.

2. Angelic Realm:

in the angelic realm we have been told they have three triads I will detail these for you.

The First Triad
Seraphim -

Which is Said to represent the highest order of angels in the pseudo-Dionysian hierarchic scheme and generally also in Jewish lore. The seraphim surround the throne of Glory and are known as the holy, holy, holy. They are said to be angels of love, light and fire. The ruling princes of the order have been given variously as Seraphiel, Jophiel, Metatron, Michael and originally as Satan. They are said to roar like lions.

Cherubim -

In the name as well as in concept, the cherubim are Assyrian or Akkadian in origin. The word means "one who prays" or "one who intercedes," Also to mean knowledge. They symbolised God's highest potencies, sovereignty, and goodness. Chief rulers are Ophaniel, Rikbiel, Cherubiel, Raphael, Gabriel, Zophiel and Satan. They are said to sound the 4 trumpets heralding the apocalypse. They are angels of light, glory, and keepers of the celestial records, the cherubim excel in knowledge.

Thrones - They rank 3rd in the 1st triad of the celestial hierarchy. The ruling prince of this angelic order is variously given as Oriphiel, Zabkiel, Zaphkiel, they are known as many-eyed ones. They bring Gods justice to bear upon us.

The Second Triad
Dominions -

They are said to regulate angel duties and are perpetually aspiring to true lordship. Through them the majesty of god is manifested. They are also known as lords and dominations. They inhabit the level where the spiritual and physical planes begin to merge and are said to regulate the duties of angelic choirs below them. Chief of the order is given as Hashmal or Zadkiel.

Virtues the principal duty of the virtues is to work miracles on earth. They are said to be the chief bestowals of grace and valour. Among the ruling princes of the order are Michael, Raphael, Barbiel, Uzziel, Peliel and originally Satan. They inspire valour in heroes and grace in saints.

Powers - Known as the Lords hosts. The principal task of the powers is to see to it that order is imposed on the heavenly pathways. They are said to stop the efforts of demons who would overthrow the world. They are also known as divine logos, creative power, sovereign power, mercy, legislation, and punitive power. Camael is commonly designated chief.

The Third Triad
Principalities -
They are known as protectors of religion and watchers over the leaders of people, they help leaders make right decisions. They are also known as the elohim. The chief ruling angels of the order are Requel, Anael, Haniel, Cerviel, and Nisroc.

Archangels - The ruling seven are known as Uriel, Raguel, Michael, Seraqael, Gabriel, Haniel, Raphael. The ruling prince is either known as Michael or Raphael. They are known as messengers bearing divine decrees from high.

Angels - The word angel derives from angiras (Sanskrit), a divine spirit also meaning courier, Greek meaning messenger. A supernatural being intermediate between God and man. They are said to be most involved with humanity, guiding and protecting us. They can not interfere with our destinies.

But instead of trying to remember all these angel triads and who this one represents etc. how about going about it the simplest way. CALL ON THE LORDS OF FLAME AND LIGHT. These lords will delegate an appropriate angel to help us with our plight.

3. Devic Kingdom:

This represents Mother Deva This realm is also known as the Arch High. They are responsible for creation with God. The Deva's are the guardians of the elements, spirits and humankind. They live among us, with their abilities lying dormant until humankind has reached a certain stage of evolution and at that time they will guide the element and further our spiritual development.

Mother Deva helps us with prophecy to do with our planet as anything that would affect planet Earth is known by the Devas.

4. Cosmic consciousness:

This applies to the universe as distinct from just planet earth. So the big picture can be ascertained from this consciousness and all other realms are ruled by the cosmic consciousness. So once you have connected with this consciousness you then can reach the oneness

5. Oneness - this is when all 4 realms work in unison.

Angels are here for many reasons and purposes, they help to keep after life secrets safe during Mediumship communications, for example. in order to make sure that certain information that we are not ready to learn is not passed over, because lets face it, if you were having a tough time, and you learnt all the wonderful secrets of the afterlife, what would you do? Would you want to stay here and suffer? Or go and see this fabulous place for yourself? Angels also help to keep us safe and to make sure that we stay on track, also for healing and for protection. But you must remember that your angel is not a fairy godmother or "cosmic vending Machine" they can however help us in many ways that are overlooked by most of us .they are the messengers of the Divine, the All, the absolute Source, and universal Law. They are not part of a single church but are of the entire reality. The benefits of communication are wonderful beyond words. they can help you work through emotional blocks and inspire you to create new circumstances they can help you to see and understand the ways in which you may be hurting yourself or preventing benefits from occurring in your life. Angels will not help you to accomplish anything that will harm yourself or others. Angels Help mostly by sending information either communicating directly if you are able to receive or indirectly with omens etc. (books fall off shelves in my path a lot for example). They can also send information in dreams and as compressed energy that unfolds over time. And by sending you very advanced healing energies using what is called Shakti, that is, a frequency or carrier of divine or spiritual intelligence and healing energy. If you are able to feel subtle energies you may feel this as warmth or tingling pulses of energy moving through your body. Everyone can benefit from working with angels, so welcome your angel to work together with you and it will create great value and personal joy in your life. Because of free will your angels can not intervene and help you unless you ask, the only exception to this is if you are involved in a life or death situation before your time. Every human without exception has, from birth at least 2 angels, who are with you all the time, and nothing that you say or do will stop them from being with you, ever. Other angels are around you, and for them to help, again all you have to do is ask!

Who and what are Angels?

As we are made of carbon and water, Angels are made of love and light energies they are also on a different evolutionary stream to humans. You will find that Fairies, Devas and elementals are also part of the angelic realm although they are not yet angels.

Angels are neither male nor female, however they are often referred to as he or she. This is a man made thing, as it makes it easier for us mere mortals to relate to them better They do not have a human form because they are made up of energy, love and light. But Angels will project themselves to us in a manner we are most comfortable with which means we often see them as human. If they have a message to give us, they may even come to us in the form of a departed loved one, so as not to scare us. Other ways Angels appear to us is through lights, colours, sounds, feelings, and scents. they have never incarnated in human form (except where mentioned) and they never will, and neither will we ever become angels. They come from the Elemental Kingdom. Angels resonate pure unconditional love.

There are very many angels around us, in fact there is at least one angel for everything that we may need during our life times, and beyond!, They represent archetypal energies, seeing as they have been around for so long, and I honestly believe that it does not matter whether or not you have memorised their names or not, if you know what kind of energy you are looking for simply ask, for example, if you need a healing angel, just call for the Angel of healing and they will come. Guardian Angels are like all other Angels, with one exception - they've been assigned to stand by us throughout our life, through good and bad. Everyone is given at least two Guardian Angels, some people, such as Light workers have more. Your Guardian Angels know everything you've said, done or thought since the day you were born. They are non-judgmental and they look forward to helping you when requested. Communicating with your Guardian Angel is not difficult. There's no magic formula, it doesn't matter if you've done "wrong" or you don't go to church regularly - they just have to be asked. There are many ways to communicate with your Angels, no method is better than the other; it just depends on what you're comfortable with. Contacting your guardian Angels is the same as contacting other Angels. All you need to do is call them.

Ascended Masters, Elementals and Fairies

Have you ever walked though a park or through the woods and felt a sudden sense of peace, a sense of peace that puts all your daily problems into balance? If this is true for you then the chances are that you have had some kind of contact an "Elemental". Elementals are "Nature's Angels" and they are referred to by various names including

Fairies, Elves, Divas, Brownies, and Leprechauns, Gnomes, Sprites, Pixies as well as many others. We have all heard of them however most of us put them down to our childhood "fairy stories" the ones that our parents may have read us,, but these elementals are not just things of so called make believe, they are real! These nature spirits are governed by the Archangels. Like Angels, Elementals do not have a definite form or appearance. It's easy to determine if a picture is that of an Angel or a winged elemental. The winged elementals have butterfly looking wings and Angels have feathered bird wings. If they choose to show themselves to you, they may choose a form that you will recognize and be comfortable with or will associate with the element they represent. A fire elemental may appear as a spark, a face in a candle flame or bonfire, or simply a sudden warm spot. A Water elemental may be a cold spot. An air elemental could be a sudden breeze or tiny whirlwind in the dust. A smell, taste, or an unexplained pebble in your shoe could be evidence of the earth elementals at play.

Elementals are very mischievous and like to play, but their play may appear to us as disasters rather than play, such as thunderstorms, blizzards, raging seas. When Elementals decide to enjoy themselves, it's best for us humans to take cover and hope they tire soon. Contrary to how it seems, Elementals activities are not always destructive, even though it may seem that way to humans at times. The elementals have their own agenda and they have a definite purpose, which we may not understand, but may be for the good of the planet as a whole.

There is a group of Elementals for each of the elements - Earth, Air, Water and Fire. Below is a brief description of some, but not all, creatures of the four elements.

Elements and their Creatures

Earth: Gnomes

Being of the earth, Gnomes usually live in the soil, rocks, beneath the ground, and under the tree roots. Gnomes will only help humans if they have been considerate of nature and treat it well. They are very helpful of those who have established a connection with them through prior acts of kindness.

The subgroups of the Earth Gnomes consist of Brownies, Dryads,

Durdalis, Earth Spirits, Elves, Hamadryads, Pans, Pygmies, Sylvestres, and Satyrs.

Air: Sylphs

The sylphs are the air spirits. Their element has the highest vibratory rate. They are said to live on the tops of mountains. The leader of the sylphs is a being called Paralda who is said to dwell on the highest mountain of Earth. They often assume human form but only for short periods of time. They are usually seen with wings, looking like cherubs or fairies. Because of their connection to air, which is associated with the mental aspect, one of their functions is to help humans receive inspiration. The sylphs are drawn to those who use their minds, particularly those on creative arts. Sylphs are usually sympathetic of human endeavours and for the most part their actions towards them are kindly and thoughtful. The Sylphs can have a profound and powerful influence on the human mental body and thought, and, they are responsible for being the primary impetus behind both inspirational art and inventions

Water: Undines

The water spirits are called Undines. They closely resemble humans in appearance and size, except for those inhabiting smaller streams and ponds. They are beautiful, emotional, and graceful Nature Spirits who dress themselves in greenish, sea colored garb that has both a shimmering consistency and a watery texture. Their ruler is known as Necksa who they love, serve, and honour unceasingly. Since their purpose is to direct the flow and course of the waters of the planet, they live in coral caves, fountains, lakes, marshlands, rivers, seas, waterfalls, and underneath lily pads. Besides caring for plants both above and below the surface of the water, the Undines are concerned with the movements of water and how they relate to human emotions and soul responses. The Undines and their subgroups are friendly, approachable, and are very willing to work with people and to help them. Etheric in nature, they exist within the water itself and this is why they can't be seen with the normal physical vision.

The subgroups of the Water Undines consist of Limoniades, Mermaids, Naiads, Oceanid, Oreads, Potamides, and Sea Maids.

Fire: Salamanders

The salamanders are the spirit of fire. Without these beings, fire cannot exist. You cannot light a match without a salamander's being present. They are considered the strongest and most powerful of all the elementals. Their ruler is a magnificent flaming being called Djin. On the spiritual level, they also help to awaken Kundalini. Salamanders will always help people who are friendly towards them and keep their heart fires burning.

Ascended Masters

So, what or who is an Ascended Master, I hear you ask ! well, an Ascended Master is a person, who has once walked the earth, as a human being which could have been in the form of a teacher, a healer or a prophet, and is now in the spirit world, where the Ascended master continues his or her work from the other side. The Ascended Master is a very powerful being, they could come from any race, religion and ethnic background and could be from Ancient times or modern times, including from our life time, I have heard it said on many quarters that there is a strong belief that our very own Princess Diana is an Ascended Master, other examples of Ascended Masters would be, Jesus, Buddha, Gandhi, Martin Luther King Jr, as well as other saints, Gods, Goddesses and other Deities.

So how would you make contact with an Ascended Master? Well that is easy, it's the same as with the Angels, you just ask ! Ascended Masters can be called upon whenever you need them, to ask for assistance with a challenging problem, for guidance in a difficult area, for example if you were suffering from writers block, call upon Walt Whitman or perhaps Elizabeth Barrett Browning but always be sure to call upon them with an open heart.

There are of course certain Ascended Masters that can be called upon to help us with specific areas, I will give you some examples of these now, but please remember this list is not inclusive, it is simply a list of the better known Ascended Masters.

Buddha – from Asia – for Balance, inner peace and joy, Spiritual Growth and understanding.

Despite being born into wealth Buddha was intent and focused on helping the poor and less fortunate, he began teaching about detachment from suffering, through realising ones inner peace, thus the foundation for Buddhism.

Brigit – Installs courage in females, helps you to find your life purpose and direction, for protection, installs warmth in all relationships,

She is the female equivalent to Archangel Michael she is also a highly respected Celtic Goddess. She is a Sun Goddess and as such is associated with fire.

Ganesha - from India, for Abundance, prosperity, healing of animals, children and fertility, working with the elemental kingdom, self-esteem.

This Ascended Master is a deity with a prominent elephant head and works to remove any blocks for those who call on him,

Isis, from Egypt, for Divine Magic, Feminine strength courage and power, for beauty, happiness and self esteem.

Also known as the Egyptian Goddess of the moon, She also assists those in crossing over.

Isolt – for reviving passion, assists with the healing of break-ups, separations and divorce, attracting romance

Isolt is known as the Goddess of Love and passion as well as enhancing sexual satisfaction and the assistance of finding your soul mate .

Kuan–Yin for Mercy, assists in Clairvoyance and compassion, installs feminine grace and power, developing musical abilities

Kuan yin has been known for her deep love for humanity and spirituality so as to enlighten others and reduce suffering.

Chapter 2
Walking With Angels

Angel communication

So what would you say if you found out that angels are actually very interested in your life, and they were just waiting for you to ask them to be part of it? What if the angels wanted to communicate with YOU?

Well they do! It's true; angels bring a profound feeling of love and support. So what are some simple steps you can do to open the doors of communication with your own angels?

Just Talk

It is really just that simple. Start talking to your angels. I started off by just talking out loud to my angels while I was doing the housework and pottering around. I found that the more I talked to my angels, the more smoothly things seemed to go for me. And yes, I did feel rather silly at the time, but no one else was around, and anyway, as my life started to improve, and I felt as though I was receiving my answers, I did start to feel less silly until talking to them became a way of life, besides, you do not have to talk out loud, you can always use thought to talk to them.

Ask

Yes that's right, that's all there is to it. Ask for help. Ask for guidance. Ask for support and peace. The angels can't intervene in our lives unless we ask; we are beings with freewill and are here to live our own lives! We have to ask for what we want.

Listen

You do not need to be psychic to hear messages from your angels. Angels can communicate with us in ways that we understand. Angels communicate with us by placing synchronicities in our path. A synchronicity is a "meaningful coincidence," and those meaningful coincidences bring us messages. Say you are thinking about moving to Australia, so you ask the angels for guidance. Then the next day you talk to a co-worker who says they went to Australia on holiday and loved it so much they wished they could move there. Coincidence? Nope, that's a synchronicity, and synchronicities can appear in many ways; a song on the radio, a phrase in an overheard conversation, a book that attracts your attention at the bookstore, or a comment from a friend.

Receive

This sounds simple, but you'd be surprised how quickly we can ask for something, only to close down with fear and worry that it won't happen for us like we want it to. If we ask for help finding a new job, then get anxious and worried and start randomly applying for jobs that we know wouldn't be any good for us, we are taking over, aren't we? Familiar with the phrase "Let Go and Let God?" That's what receiving is all about. If you are trying to solve your problems by charging in on your white horse, then you are not being open to receive, but are trying to control your situation out of fear. When we are truly open to receive, we are letting our path unfold before us and trusting that things will work out. We need to truly hand our problems over to the angels, and then let go and let them do what they will.

Have Faith

We need to have faith that the angels are behind the scenes working things out for us. If we don't have faith, we are pushing away everything that the angels are pushing toward us. Sometimes it can be hard to have faith, so if you feel yourself getting fearful ask the angels for faith and patience that things will be okay. And it's okay to keep asking for faith! When I'm short on faith, I like to recite the following prayer:

The Prayer of Faith

By Hannah More Kohaus God is my help in every need;God does my every hunger feed;God walks beside me, guides my wayThrough every moment of the day.I now am wise, I now am true,Patient, kind and loving, too.All things I am, can do, and be,Through Christ, the Truth that is in me.God is my health, I can't be sick;God is my strength, unfailing, quick;God is my all, I know no fear,Since God and love and Truth are here.

Be Thankful

Thank the angels for everything as if it's already all worked out! Honestly in the mind of the Divine, everything IS already all worked out. It just may take a little time to manifest for you to see it in physical form. So be very thankful! The angels are working very hard for you.

Working with the angels is really very simple, and the benefits are never ending. When we open our hearts and minds, the angels can truly work miracles in our lives. Angels communicate with us using subtle methods. Often, when we ask angels for help we will maybe turn on the radio or television and hear or see something which answers our question perfectly. We might meet a stranger in the street who comes up to us, says exactly what we need to hear then walks off. This is likely to be an angel working through that person.

There are many ways the angels can connect to us. Once you call on your angels, they are there, whether or not you sense or feel them. We always receive the help we ask for. We just need to be open to receive it.

Help from the angels can come in many forms. One way we can receive the guidance of the angels is through our feelings. We may get that gut feeling, an intuition, get chills or shivers in our body, or we may just feel the angels energy around us. It is very important to trust these feelings and not discard them because they are just "feelings". This is a very important way that angels communicate with us.

Another way the angels communicate with us is through our dreams or visions. This is a way of "seeing" the guidance of the angels. If you are a visual person, images may come to mind that give you clarity or guidance about your request for help. It may be a different way of seeing the issue, or a new perspective that you hadn't seen before. Trust what you see. If you're not sure, ask for clarification or a sign from the angels. Again, be open to receive further clarification and understanding. I will go into this further in the next part of this chapter

If you are an auditory person, you may receive your messages through hearing. You may mentally hear a voice or words. The angels' words are always loving and positive. They will never say anything negative, so if you are hearing negative words, it may be your own self-talk. It is important to differentiate between the two so you can easily identify the voice of the angels.

How Can I Detect Angelic Presence?

There are a number of ways of detecting angelic presence, some generic, and some specific to individual angels. Angels will appear in ways that we as individuals are comfortable with but some of the most common or universally experienced signs are:-

- An overwhelming feeling of love and joy
- Changes in temperature
- Simply 'knowing' that an Angel is near
- Feeling protected and safe
- 'Angelic' music with no source (rare)
- 'Angelic' fragrance with no source (rare)

- Coloured Light(s) - especially white, purple or gold
- Feathers

Feathers are the most common sign and they are recognised by most people as an angel's 'calling card' (even though they do not actually have wings). As such, do not expect your feather to be a beautiful large white 'angel' feather, the angels will use whatever is around. How will you know if it is an angelic calling card or just a random feather? Was your attention drawn to that feather? Then it was meant for you! If calling on angels in meditation, it is common for angels to stand in front of or completely surround the meditator and channel their messages from their heart to the meditator's heart. (Unlike for example, ascended masters or spirit guides who usually stand behind and channel information into the crown chakra). Another way of detecting whether or not you are in touch with angels is that the messages they give are always full of hope and love and are very positive (again, unlike ascended masters and spirit guides who, while always encouraging and positive, may give you a 'telling off' if they feel you need it!) Angels will also sometimes show themselves in aura photographs as balls of white light and some individuals have even been lucky enough to capture them in normal photographs.

Symbols and Dreams

Dreams are an important tool that your guardian Angel uses to communicate with you, your Angels communicates with your higher self, your soul, and this information filters directly to your inner knowing, your wisdom, the messages that your Angels want to give you can come in different ways, one of the more well know is Symbolic form , As you can imagine symbols in dreams have been identified and referred to throughout the world. These symbols can include tornadoes, climbing stairs, falling from a height or running. As you would expect there are other symbols in dreams that have special meanings that allow us to interpret and analyze our dreams. When you see these symbols in your dreams you need to look at what context the symbols were presented to you so you can then analyse what the symbol was trying to mean.

Animals in dreams might refer to our own animal instincts where once we were great hunters and now we are not. We can interpret this to mean that we want to be more aggressive with our lives, not angry, but to seek a fulfilling life and become a real go-getter. The exact interpretation of an animal dream depends on the type of animal in the dream.

Angels in your dreams are very important symbols. Angels do come in different colours and the colour does mean something relative to the angel. Each colour represents the angel to be symbols of knowledge, wholesomeness or integrity. The appearance of angels in a dream can be an illustration for spiritual integrity, a desire to improve your live. Angels in your dreams often means you are being provided with a message or a direction your life needs to take.

Altars: Dreaming about an altar tends to symbolize that a project you've been working on will be successful. If there are lighted candles on your altar is a double sign of success. Kneeling in front of the altar suggests you are a deeply spiritual person, and that divine intervention will assist in your success.

Dancing in a dream can offer a variety or reasons, depending on the features of the dance and its perspective as dancing can be a symbol for romance or sex. Dancing in a dream can also be a symbol of freedom.

Bags: The dream Bag contains character and personality traits that either hinder or help you. As such, it is necessary to pay attention to what is hiding in the Bag. When a Bag occurs in our dreams, it is a message to search our unconscious deeper to uncover what is blocking us or what is supporting us. By identifying these things we are able to accelerate our growth

Black Dreams with a symbol of black is often interpreted to mean the end of something. The colour black in our times is a symbol for death, such as funerals etc. Now seeing black symbols in your dream does not mean you are going to die but it means the end of something. Perhaps you have been troubled by an issue and when you have dreamt about it you saw black. This would indicate to you that your dream is for you to consider terminating that issue, bring it to an end.

Blood being seen in your dream often means that you hold or want to have supremacy and liveliness. Seeing blood in your dream does not mean exactly one thing, but it is the scenario that your dream played when you saw the blood. During times of stress or some traumatic event in your life you might see blood in your dream meaning the situation has become out of control or reflects the despair you are feeling. If you see your hands and there is blood on them you may very well be suffering a terrible feeling of guilt.

Cars being in your dreams often means freedom, driving a car you are in complete control and can travel to wherever you choose. The opposite can be said if the driving is erratic and out of control, a complete reflection of your life.

Clocks: The dream Clock, as you would guess, deals with time. Specifically, the Clock may indicate that you are afraid that life is moving by you, or things are moving too fast. If you are dreaming that you are winding a Clock, this means that you may be starting a new phase in your life, or heading in a new direction. If the Clock alarms then you are faced with a life-changing decision.

Devils: The Devil in dreams symbolizes darkness and confusion. Its dreamtime visitation may also mean you are preoccupied with negative thoughts, or someone in your life is bringing you down to a negative emotional level. The Devil may also indicate you are dealing with temptations. The Devil is also the personification of ego - it may be time to soften your ego a bit.

Eyeglasses: Dream symbol meaning for Eyeglasses deals with how you see things in your world. If you are wearing Eyeglasses in your dream it is a symbol of moderation, balance, and virtue. If you've lost your Eyeglasses, you are going need to be aware of lies being told in your life, and some unsolved mysteries may be coming your way. If you dream of Eyeglasses by themselves, it may mean you have a distorted view of your world and surroundings at this time.

Eggs are where life emanates from and means birth. Eggs can mean that you have taken a new path in life, totally changing the way you were or could indicate to you your level of contentment. The opposite can be said if the egg is in pieces, reflecting your life beliefs and faiths.

Fog is a difficult symbol as it could mean you cannot see clearly the direction in your life or the answer to an issue. Being in a fog you cannot see where to go and causes you to be confused where on the other hand you have to get out of the fog and take a new path in areas you are unfamiliar with.

Forest: Have you heard the adage: "can you see the Forest for the trees?" Dream Forests deal with experience, vision, emotions and shadows. Forests in our dreams may indicate unresolved feelings about something, or not being able to see our way clear of a problem. Forests may indicate we feel lost in our lives. On the other hand, if you are dreaming of a beautiful, lush Forest, this indicates an unshakable faith in the Divine and prosperity is your destiny. Seeing a Forest fire indicates health problems.

Gate as you know is one way in or one way out. During your dream see which way it was that you went through the gate. It might mean you are entering a new phase or leaving one.

House: Dream symbol meaning for House deals with the body, as well as a desire for security and safety. The condition of the House in your dream represents how you truly feel about your current situation. If the House is in ill-repair or disarray, you need to take a close look at your health. If you are building a House, you should expect visits from old friends and you'll make new friends. A picture-perfect House means you are ready to settle down into a more stable situation.

Illness in your dream is a very important symbol. If the illness is about you then that means a trip to your doctor. You might have suspected an illness and your dream is confirming it to you.

Keys depict opening and closing. You lock the door or you have opened the door. Once locked whatever is behind that door stays there and no one else sees it. It might mean that you are behind that locked door living life you don't want anyone else to see or you have a secret.

Mask: Dream Masks deal with the inability to be comfortable with being ourselves. When we dream of Masks, it often infers that we are not comfortable in our own skin, or we are incapable of showing others our true selves. Often, Masks represent overuse of drugs, alcohol or food to cover up our emotions. If others are wearing Masks in your dreams, it may mean that others are not being fully honest with you.

Mountain: Mountains in our dreams symbolize conquering, overcoming, hard work, willpower, and ascending above petty circumstances. Climbing the Mountain implies hard work in learning a new skill. Descending the Mountain implies stepping back from a situation, taking time to think about your actions, getting a second opinion. A Mountain range in your dream represents a new adventure, and is a message encouraging expansion in your life

Owls are wise and a dream of owls indicates you want to seek more information or to understand a situation better so you can make an informed decision.

Road as you would expect is leading to somewhere. There are straight and winding roads, steep or downhill slope roads. Roads generally depict the direction your life is taking.

Rings: Dream rings represent a promise or bond we have with our destiny, with another person, or with our community. This symbolic bond is incredibly strong and infinite. When we dream of a Ring slipping off our finger, we must rekindle the relationships we've let slip. When we dream of Rings that are stuck on our finger, we need to re-examine an unhealthy relationship

Stairs Dreams of climbing stairs similar to mountains except this is all about where you stand in life. Are you reaching the heights you should be reaching or are you going down the stairs where your life is not reaching your expectations.

Shoes: Shoe dreams deal with walking certain paths in our lives. If you are wearing tight Shoes, the road you are travelling is hard, and much sorrow is involved. Comfortable Shoes indicate you are in a good place in your life and success is around the corner. Buying Shoes indicates you still have quite a distance to travel until you reach your goals. Dirty, worn-down Shoes encourage us to examine our spiritual walk, or asks us to take a walk of faith.

Tunnel: Dream symbol meaning of Tunnels deals with birth, and sometimes death. Tunnels in our dreams ask us to look back to a starting point. In Tunnels we often encounter our deepest mind - our unconscious thoughts. Tunnels encourage us to follow a path into the unknown. They are a message for us to begin exploring our own concepts of life, death, and birth.

Umbrella: Umbrellas in our dreams indicate our need to take a closer look at our worries and fears. When we have an open Umbrella in our dream we must act carefully and watch how we behave with others. A closed Umbrella means we are worrying and obsessing unnecessarily. When Umbrellas appear, we must ask what we are afraid of because our fears are holding us back from progress.

Water: Dream symbol meaning of Water deals with cleansing and emotional stirrings. If the Water is murky in your dream, this is a warning not to get involved in new endeavours. If the Water is clear, success is coming your way. Seeing yourself in Water's reflection means that you aren't being fully honest with yourself. When you contemplate your dream of Water, keep in mind Water is a symbol of your emotional state.

In conclusion then, if any of the above symbols are in your dreams, you now know what they may mean and can interpret successfully your dream analysis.

Opening up to Angels

There is always so much written and said about how you should open yourself up to Angels, but what can be certain is that everyone has their own unique way of doing so, what may work perfectly for one may not work for another, so if you have taken advise from a friend, or maybe a book about how to open up, and you find that you' just do not get it' do not be disheartened, you are not "just one person that can not do it" just try another way, until you find a method that "feels right"

Angels naturally answer you and will draw closer to you the more you speak to them, they are influenced by your power of intention, Performing some sort of ritual can add power to that intention, but if you do not feel comfortable with rituals you will be pleased to know that it is not essential, Angels will answer you and be there for you, no matter what.

Angels, as I have said earlier are not allowed to interfere in your life without being invited to, by you. Neither are they able to do anything that is not for your highest good, or for the highest good of any other that may be involved. They are also not allowed to interfere in your Karma in any way, however they can and will guide you through whatever issues you came into this life to face.

How often you communicate with your Angels, and with what you ask them to help you with, is up to you, you may be sceptical at first, or you may be thinking, "why would an Angel be bothered with little unimportant me?" or you may feel that your problem or issue is not important enough to bother the Angels with, but you would be wrong! They can't wait to help you, and any issue that affects you, is important enough,

Working with Angels can bring a dramatic change in your life. Not only on the outside but on the inside too, once you have invited the angels into your life you will start to see the signs of their help. One of the first things that you may encounter are white feathers, they can seem to just drift and fall in front of you, outside in the street or while indoors, they come to tell you that you are not alone and that your angel is there with you. Or they may come as confirmation that you have made the right decision to praise you for getting it right. Remember, whenever you find a feather do not forget that it is there for a reason,

There are Angels for everything and they are just waiting for us to ask for their help. They can't help if we don't ask. Our request doesn't have to be long and lengthy. It can be quite short to be affective. This is always a fun exercise until you are more comfortable with asking for what it is you need help with : Next time you head out for the shopping centre while you are on route ask the parking Angels for help." Parking Angels I need a parking place close to the door and with good lighting (if at night) and I would appreciate your help." Be sure and say "Thank you " and let it go. When you get to your destination watch what happens! This is always fun for kids to get involved with and gets them used to asking for an Angel's help. When you get comfortable with asking for the small stuff then start asking for more help in bigger situations in your life. You can ask an Angel's help for anything. Finding the right job, the house at a price that you can afford, help in getting a new car, a relationship, the right doctor, computer. There is help just waiting. Be sure you get specific in the details in what you want or you can wind up getting a new home not close enough to work or the amount of bedrooms you really need. The help you ask for can be tangible and intangible things. Remember to always thank the Angels for their assistance and they will never get tired of helping you.

Just ask. The Angels are waiting to assist you in all of life's moments

Asking the Angels for help

Asking an Angel for help is one of our most power spiritual practices. We can ask the Angels for immediate help at any time and in any place. A Jewish proverb says that "Every blade of grass has an Angel bending over it saying. 'Grow, Grow!" Just as every person has one or more Guiding Angels that help and assist them, every human activity partnerships, businesses, organizations and relationships - also have one or more Angels that preside over offerings of grace, assistance and blessings for them. Call upon your Angels whenever you are need. Here are some tips that will help you:

Seven Tips For Connecting With Your Angels

Ask for help – Angels offer us help 24/7; the more receptive we are, the more help they can give us. If you diminish your receptivity you limit the Angels ability to help you. Create your own invocations, or prayers, that specifically call for the help you need. Realise that when you call upon an Angel, that what really happens is that you open yourself into greater receptivity to their assistance. Further down in this chapter I include some different ways of invoking that work for me.

Realise yourself as fully worthy of Angelic assistance. Angels work with everyone regardless of personal histories and beliefs. Angels are infinite and omnipresent – your request does not diminish them in anyway nor does it affect there ability to be with and help everyone else at the same time. They exist beyond our experience of time and space. They respond to everyone with complete unconditional love.

Connect with your inner divine child as you call upon the Angels and ask for help. Your inner divine child is whole, innocent and true - and recognises Angels as true and trustworthy gifts of Creator. This will help create openness, receptivity, excitement, eagerness and wonder as you prepare to receive the gift your Angels have prepared for you.

Hand everything over to the Angels during your time of invocation and prayer. Every issue, problem, worry and fear as well as every good intention and positive outcome you imagine as the result of your request. Release all expectations of how your request will be answered.

Express Appreciation and Gratitude – Find and express genuine appreciation and gratitude for things exactly as they are. If you are struggling with this, ask the Angels to help you to find the love that is present in whatever difficulty you are facing. Have patience with this and let go of any expectation of how the love may be revealed to you.

Know that it is done – Every prayer is answered and grace is always given. If you fear that your prayer will not be answered, then ask for help in understanding and seeing more clearly. Trust that you will see the love in every answered prayer. You are known completely and loved unconditionally by the Angels and nothing that will serve you is ever withheld from you.

Act quickly on the guidance you receive – accept the opportunity and act upon it immediately. Angelic help is infinite and unlimited – you can not use it up or run out of it. You cannot ask for 'too much' and the Angels are joyously happy to give to you without limit. The faster you act, the faster you receive more assistance!

Celebrate yourself exactly as you are in the moment. Leave any critical judgments or negative feelings about yourself, your life, or others in the hands of the Angels for healing. Even if it is just for a few moments, let go of everything that is not of love for yourself and everything around you. In this moment of surrender much more can done for you by the Angels than you can accomplish on your own. Thank yourself and the Angles for deepening and the relationship between you.

As we have mentioned earlier, there are angels for just about every task that you could think of. There are angels in charge of our waterways, angels who watch over the passage of the moon and angels in charge of things such a world peace. There are even angels that can help you to move house and write letters! So please do not be afraid of asking an angel for help. You won't be taking them away from a greater task. Angels are not ruled by time and space in the way that we are, and can easily be in many places at once. If you need an angel's help, just ask.

Here is a list of common problem areas and the angels that you can call upon to help you.

Life Problem	Your Angel Helper
Animals	Ariel
Calculations	Raziel
Childcare and pregnancy	Sandalphon and Raphael
Communicating	Gabriel and Metatron
Developing Psychically	Jeremiel
Disagreements	Raguel, Gabriel
Finding lost things	Chamuel
Grieving and illness	Raphael and Azrael
Inspiration and Creating things	Jophiel and Gabriel
Living Accommodation	Chamuel
Memory	Haniel
Outdoor spaces	Uriel
Romance	Haniel
Safety	Michael
Travelling	Raphael
Worry about cash flow	Michael

Communicating with your angels is a personal thing but it is useful to have a place to start! Here are some ideas to inspire you.

1. Write down the name of the angel you need on a piece of paper. Place it under your pillow last thing at night. That way you will be 'sleeping' on the task at hand. Ask the angels to help you morning and night until you see your way clear.

2. Print out the name of your angel on a piece of card (the size of a business card) and have it laminated. Carry it with you in a wallet or purse and every time you look at the card it will bring your request to the front of your mind, keeping your helper's name freshly in your mind.

3. Use a picture or postcard of an angel as a focus for your request. Write down your problem on the back of the card. This literally and

symbolically leaves the angel 'on top' of the problem.

You don't have to use any specific words or phrases to do this and sometimes it is better to work 'from the heart.' But always write your request in such a way that it seems as if the problem has already been solved.

Use the phrase, 'Thank you angels for helping me solve this problem.'

Did you know that angels can help with our hobbies and even assist us in the workplace? Each angel has guardianship over different types of skills. The Archangel Gabriel is one of the better known angels and it is the angel Gabriel who went to Mary to give her the news that she was carrying the baby Jesus. Forever after, Gabriel was associated with the role of communicator. Gabriel is the patron of postal workers and in fact all communicators!

The Archangel Michael has long been associated with protection and guardianship. Paintings and statues the world over feature Michael carrying a flaming sword, and often dressed ready for battle. Michael is the patron of police officers, and the armed forces, for obvious reasons! You don't need to belong to a large organisation to call on these angels for help. Angels help anyone, any time and anywhere. Although some people prefer to call on the angels using specific rituals and practices, it is ok to do what feels right for you. If you like to pray to your angels every night before you go to bed then do that. If you find it easier to talk to your angels whilst you are out in nature, then that's fine too. Do you like to meditate at home on your own? Or ask your angels to give you a message in your dreams? My own angels nearly always communicate with me in that way!

If you can't remember the right angel for the job, don't worry. Just ask for '...the best angel for the task,' and the right angel will be found for you. Know it will be done. Let the angels find a solution for you - they often come up with something much better than we can think of on our own!

Angel Healing

So what is Angel Healing I hear you ask, Well Angel healing is simply a restoration of the inner balance, be it your emotions, your health or even some life situations, It can cleanse the aura, releasing blockages that will help to heal issues of the past as well as to give more clarity on the present. It is such a relaxing treatment that you can easily drift off to sleep knowing that you are wrapped up in the wings of the angels, It releases pain and sooths the mind and body. When we ask the Angels to restore the Harmony within us they will be there in an instant.

A typical healing session lasts for around 45 minutes, during the treatment the Angel Practitioner will be connecting with your Angels and the Archangelic realm asking them to bestow healing on you while the healing is taking place, you may experience heat, cold, tingling sensations, you may see colours, see visions or even receive helpful guiding messages. After the healing has taken place many clients express a deep sense of clam, peace and contentment.

You must always remember that this is not a "miracle cure" Angelic healing will not and does not substitute medical care or advice, so please note that I am not a doctor and can not diagnose any physical diseases . Angels on request will always heal what needs to be healed to restore your complete balance, as long as it is for the higher good of everybody, but always bear in mind that sometimes we need to pass certain lessons in our lives, and then, the angels can not interfere with this, but whatever the problem is you can be sure that the Angels will always help to sooth the pain, or solve the situation, even if they can not interfere with this particular lesson.

Angel healing does not have to be done in person, it can also be done distantly, it does not matter which method you choose as in reality, and we are all one.

There are many different types of healing, such as Reiki, Kundalini, Seichem, Spiritual Healing and Quantum touch, although they may sound as if they are different in my opinion they are all essentially the same, as they all connect to the higher realm, the methods and vibrations may be different but they all connect to the same energy. The only difference is the strength of energy that the healer can channel, which of course depends on how clear a channel the healer is, and how much healing the healer has done, the channels are cleared in the healer by several methods, the main one I believe is the attunments received, the amount of their own issues they have managed to release, which again I believe is helped immensely by the attunments and training process, which is why I feel finding the right teacher and Healing master is essential if you wish to be a strong, clear healer.

For those of you who wish to feel the energy of channelling Healing energy for the first time you may try the method below which I have found to be the simplest way to channel healing energy, but please remember that if you wish to be a strong clear channel I would advise you to locate a good healing master that will attune you and work with you to explain and teach you the best methods.

Open your Chakras
Place protection around yourself and your client
Hold your arms out in front of you with your palms facing upwards
Ask for the healing energy to be connected to you
At this point you may feel a tingling sensation coming from your palms, you may also feel heat or cold, but do not worry if you do not, just believe and trust that the healing energy is being connected.
Place your hands on your client's body or aura, channel the energy until you feel drawn to move your hands to another area, you will be drawn to wherever the energy needs to go.

When you have finished channelling this energy remember to close your chakras and thank the Angels for channelling the energy through you. Be aware that as you are channelling the healing energy to help heal people you will also receive healing as it passes through you, and as the energy starts to cleanse and detox your body and life you may for a short while develop some physical symptoms of this, such as needing the loo more often, you may develop the symptoms of a cold, or even suffer from a head ache you can also feel emotional this is due to your body letting go of things that have been lodged in it, so do not panic, as you are releasing all this negativity and clearing your channels.

The Archangel who oversees all healing is Archangel Raphael, who is the Archangel of healing, knowledge and science. Archangel Raphael and his angels are everywhere at all times, and oversee everything to do with healing, So you can ask Archangel Raphael to assist in your healing. To connect with Archangel Raphael healing is easy; just follow the simple steps below

Connecting to Archangel Raphael

You must first open your Chakras, protect and ground yourself you will find methods of how to do this in chapter 6

Now set your intention in your mind and your heart that you intend to invoke Archangel Raphael.

Now you need to invoke him, to do this I like to keep things simple, and as I believe and trust in the power of three I like to say the following three times –

" Archangel Raphael, angel of all healing, please be with me here and now, and allow me to channel your healing for (now you could say the persons name, or read a list of names) for their highest good."

You may now notice the energy sensations travelling through you, remember that as you send healing you are also receiving healing, also as you are now connected to Archangel Raphael, you may if you wish take this opportunity to speak to him, you may wish to ask him the best way to heal a issue within yourself.

When you have received and channelled all the healing you require, or you feel the energy fade off, remember to thank Archangel Raphael for the healing and bid him farewell for now.

Focus on your breathing now, close your chakras, then you may wish to stretch yourself out,

Guardian Angels

Guardian Angels are like all other Angels, but with one difference, They have each been assigned us individually to stand by us throughout our lives, to be there through good and bad. Every one of us have been given at least 2 Guardian angels and some people such as light-workers have more. Your guardian angel knows absolutely everything about you, they know everything that you have ever said or done since the day you were born, they do not judge us and love us unconditionally , they love nothing more than to help you whenever you ask, but you do have to ask as they will not just step in without invitation. Unless it is a life or death situation.

Connecting with your guardian angel is easy, there is no magic formula, no ritual unless of course that is what you prefer. All you need to do is call them, that it, just call them, however if you do like to have some sort of a ritual, you may like to construct an Alter, or to Meditate or burn incense, there are lots of different ways people like to use, no one of these are better than the other, it is just personal preference. And although these methods may set the stage, and make the angels feel welcomed, they are not necessary, the angels do not demand this, all that is needed is a thought "angel I need your help" they will always come, If you open yourself up to their energy you will be able to feel their presence.

Once you are feeling your angels you can talk to them, ask them questions to help you, to do this, simply open yourself up, ask your questions then let your mind go blank and allow anything to flow, do not try to force it, just let it flow of its own accord. As you get to know your angels better you will soon learn how to tell them apart, you will sense their different energy's, and so you will recognise when they are close, and when you have discovered what each one specialize in, and so will be able to call that particular guardian angel to help when you need assistance in that area.

There are other ways that you may like to communicate with your guardian angels, meditation is a good way, reading Angel cards are another favourite.

We are so funny, we ask to hear our guardian angels, and when we do we start to think that we are crazy because we are hearing voices, even if we do not think that we are crazy, we will not tell anyone else for fear that they will think us crazy !

This is a favourite visualisation that I have that helps me connect to my guardian angels

Light some candles, and play some gentle music,

Visualise yourself in a beautiful garden, on a stunning summers day, the sun is shining and you can feel the warmth of the sun on your head and shoulders, you can hear the birds singing in the distance, and you can hear the gentle sounds of flowing water from what sounds like a garden water feature,

You find a bench of some sort and you take a seat, relaxed and calm you take in your surroundings, then you call for your guardian angels, you ask for your angel to come to you and let her presence be known, over in the corner near a rose bush you notice a movement, You instinctively know that this is your guardian angel, and as she draws closer, she outstretches her arms, pulls you near and hugs you close.

Ask your guardian angel her name, it might be an angelic name, it may be a common name, a exotic name or maybe something very simple, ask her a question that you truly desire the answer for, be alert for any thought patterns that you might have, feelings or visions which appear after your questions, stay with her for as long as you wish.

When you are done, hug her, thank her for her help and say goodbye for now, know that she is always with you and you can talk to her whenever you wish,

Start to wiggle your fingers and toes and become aware of the room around you, when you are ready, open your eyes.

Angel cards

Many people feel the need to work closely with their angels and guides after a mystical experience introduces them to the 'idea' of their unseen teachers and protectors. Our guides and angels can appear in dramatic ways and many visit in dreams and visions. However, not all angels work in such spectacular ways and many prefer a more subtle approach. Angel cards are a perfect way to build a relationship with your guardian angel and spirit guides.

There are many different types of Angel cards on the market, and they will all enable you to connect with your Angels, you need to get the pack that you are most drawn to, this may be the colours that draws you, maybe the pictures or it may even just be a word or description, Just ask your Angels to guide you to the correct ones for you. Trust your instincts, no matter what deck you buy, you will find that Most angel card decks contain a series of single, positive messages or simple, optimistic phrases. Interpreting them is mainly a matter of practice. My first bit of advice with using any sort of divination pack would be 'to throw away the instruction book!' Real clairvoyants and psychics work from instinct – in theory, it would be possible to use beer mats, but they're nothing like as nice to shuffle!

So, now you have your new pack, so now is the time to get to know them, they will soon feel like an old friend! So the first thing to do is to familiarise yourself with the pictures and phrases on each card. Make yourself comfortable with shuffling and laying the cards out on the table – get a real feel of your cards. Spend a little time playing with them – doing nothing in particular!

I would now at this point want to cleanse my pack, you cleanse them to get rid of any unwanted energy that may be on them, this can be done in several ways, my favourite way is to use smudge sticks Drawing the pack through the smoke of a smudge stick (sage for purification), or holding the pack over scented incense , this is the traditional method of preparing your cards. I like to work with Frankincense (a high 'vibrational' oil which is perfect for connecting to the angelic realms). Two or three drops of oil, in an oil burner is a lovely way to create the perfect atmosphere for your reading..

For safe keeping It's important to keep your angel cards in a special place. The small, single word cards are lovely in an open bowl

The larger cards deserve looking after. You can wrap you cards in a piece of silk or black velvet. If you're not clever with a needle and thread, you can easily buy lovely little drawstring pouches . If you want to keep your cards free from the energy of others, then you can pack them safely in a little wooden box after each use.

So what is a reading and how do you do them, An angel card reading consists of selecting 3 cards from the Angel card deck.

By asking the angels a question and holding that question in your mind while the card deck spreads out, you can find out "What your Angels want you to know". Or, you can simply ask the angels about life areas, ask about another person, or even ask a question on behalf of another person. It's up to you, but remember to think of your question as you select the cards.

Angelic Karma

You can also work with spreads , What's a spread? Usually, cards are laid out in spreads (in patterns on the table). Although you will find lots of different 'patterns' in books, there is no right or wrong way to do this and you can easily make up your own. With a spread, each card represents a question or part of an answer – the lay out of the cards helps you to remember which card is for which question!

Three Card Spread

A three card spread is a simple way to start. Lay your cards out in a line. The first card signifies your Past (place it furthest away from you), the middle card signifies your present (place the card in the middle) and the third card represents your future.

A Six Card Spread

Lay out cards as above. Place a second row of cards alongside the first. Each of these second cards can be used to expand on the first card...it might be the card you use to 'explain' why things happened the way they did in the past, how they are developing in the present, and as a guide to how to work out the future!

Specific Questions

Most people want to know about either love, money or work situations, or you can easily work with a single query. As with tarot cards, it is better to use at least three cards – but go ahead and use as many as you want to answer your query. You could make up your own shape spreads with each set of cards indicating certain questions. Cards in the shape of a heart might be used to answer queries about love and so on.

How to read the cards

Always follow your instincts first. Each card has many meanings. If you pick a card which says LOVE for example and you feel that the person needs to GIVE love then say so. If you feel the card means that their angel or guide is SENDING love, then say that, don't spend too much time worrying about getting it wrong, the more you practice, the stronger your links will be and the better your interpretations will be in return.

Creating Alters or Sacred Spaces

It is always nice to have that special place, that quiet place where you can talk to your angels in peace, where you can place your angel treasures, and perhaps do a little meditation while you are there, this is why angel alters are such a wonderful thing to create and build, they do not have to be expensive, a simple shelf or table will suffice, All you need is that quiet place where you can be on your own without disturbance, somewhere that is a relaxing peaceful place for you, this could even be outdoors.

As mentioned earlier, an alter does not need to cost a fortune, and you do not even need loads of space, an Alter can be an area on a coffee table, dresser or shelf, what gives it its meaning and power is your intention in creating and using it, you could place on your alter crystals which you have programmed for particular intentions, to use this method choose crystals, power animals or stones, while holding them keep your particular intention in mind as strongly as possible, for example if you want to place healing stones on your alter, while holding these crystals or stones, you may want to imaging healing symbols, or visualise someone being healed.

Other things that you could place on your Alter can be anything that represents the Angels to you, maybe some pretty feathers or shells, candles, perhaps a little angel ornament or a piece of angel jewellery, anything that you feel appropriate could go on your Alter, you can bring over time little gifts especially when you come to your alter for help, gifts like a pretty leaf, a pine cone or a flower, you can even leave them little notes to them asking for their help or asking them for their advice, you can be sure that you will receive their answer or advice either during a dream or meditation or in some other communication method or symbolic way!

Very soon you will find that when you are feeling low, you will come to this special place and it will bring you great comfort and joy and will provide a very strong link with your Angels when you need it most.

SO HOW DO YOU GO ABOUT ASSEMBLING YOUR ALTER

You should always be guided by your intuition to assemble you alter but for those who prefer more structured methods of organization, who want to begin with structure until they feel comfortable with the intuitive method, or who want to combine intuition and structure, I've listed below just a few out of the many methods. In any of these, though there are general formats, your intuition will still be involved.

The Chakra Method

One way I use is to arrange crystals by chakras. In this method I would begin with first chakra stones, followed by stones of each succeeding chakra, arranged in a circle. You can use from one to however many crystals you have free for thus purpose.

I also place crystal animals, power stones, and pocket totems in appropriate locations. For me, appropriate relates to the meaning the particular animal may have for me. An eagle, for example, means to me freedom in one's body, so my crystal eagle is grouped with the first-chakra stones. I relate elephants to communication (fifth chakra), dolphins to healing (fourth chakra), although it could as easily represent the sixth chakra (dreams, sleep, inner wisdom).

I pay special attention to what I place in the centre of the altar. For the chakra arrangement I like to have a quartz cluster or clear quartz sphere, as I feel that this radiates out energy to all of the other stones. With the cluster or sphere in the centre, I find that the arrangement seems to create a continuous flow of balancing energy.

The Four Directions/Elements

Another arrangement is to work with the four directions/four elements, as used in Celtic and Native Americans systems. In this arrangement, North is Earth, South is Fire, East is Air, and West is Water. Intuition and imagination help in assigning crystals to these values. Hematite, to me, is clearly an Earth stone; while Ruby is Fire. Aquamarine is logical for the Water area, and amethyst and lapis seem to me to signify Air. Other stones call for more subtle and subjective interpretations. Rose quartz, being related to the heart and to emotions, might belong in the Water area. Perhaps, though, the colour pink can be interpreted as soft or quiet fire. Green stones are especially interesting in terms of placement. To me, green calcite is very much a Water stone; while malachite feels earthy.

I find that what works best when I am using this method of arrangement is to experiment, moving the less obviously-related stones around until it feels that they are in the right place.

The Feng Shui Method

In using this method you treat the area which will be the surface for your fountain as if it were a room or house..

The Centre

In Feng Shui what is placed in the centre of the room or house is the most important element. I noted in the description of the chakra method that I like to put a quartz crystal or sphere in the centre.

If I'm using a crystal sphere or statue as the centre I often like to place four single-terminated points, with points facing outward, around the centrepiece. I feel that this radiates energy to the entire arrangement.

Special Kinds of Altars

An altar may be devoted to a particular purpose, such as healing, manifestation of abundance, or love (as in relationships, family harmony, etc.) In such cases you will probably choose to focus on crystals specifically related to these purposes.

Green stones are always helpful for healing, and special centre pieces might be a statue of Kwan Yin, or a green calcite or aventurine sphere.

Frogs and dolphins, both of which symbolize healing, are appropriate for this kind of altar.

For abundance (which can also use the colour green as well as yellow), an appropriate centrepiece might be a pyrite cluster.

For love we generally focus on the pink stones, and if improved communication is part of the state you wish to create you might choose to add aquamarine, chrysocolla, blue lace agate, lari-mar, turquoise, or amazonite. Helpful power animals include wolf and otter (they mate for life), and hummingbird, for the transcendent aspects of love.

Some people like to create angel altars for angelic guidance. Angelite is the most obvious stone to use, as is amethyst for its transitional quality (this stone is the colour of twilight), and rose quartz, to symbolize the unconditional love which angels have for us. Any symbols of angels work well as centrepieces.

For any of the above special altars I also like to use quartz points to direct and enhance the energy, and grounding stones (hematite, obsidian, black tourmaline, tiger's eye, or smoky quartz) to also ground the energy.

Seasonal Altars

Many people like to either vary the elements of their altars or have particular ones related to the seasons.

A winter altar might include pine cones, evergreen tree branches, and a focus on clear crystals such as quartz, calcite, danburite, and selenite. Red and green accents often brighten up a winter altar. Owl can represent the inner wisdom associated with winter; while Bear symbolizes hibernation and going within.

A spring altar would have a focus on green. A vase containing spring flowers could make a meaningful centrepiece. Green stones and green candles help to celebrate the season of renewal. The singing of spring peepers at this time makes Frog, a symbol of healing and rebirth, appropriate for this season.

For a summer altar I think most easily of the golden stones to symbolize the sun. I like to contrast these with blue stones, representing the sky and the sea. I am also drawn to the symbol of Deer, as this is the time when fawns begin to appear.

An autumn altar may include red, orange, and yellow stones. A cornucopia in which a crystal programmed for abundance is placed can make an appropriate centrepiece. The squirrel, gatherer of nuts for the coming winter, is a helpful symbol.

Enjoy creating your altar(s). You will find it to be a peaceful, meditational activity..

In my experience I've learned that one of the biggest issues people have is in the area of being grounded. Some people tell me they're earthbound; they can't seem to lift off to explore other dimensions. Others say they have wonderful visions, but experience difficulty in translating them into material terms.

The ability to be grounded is very important to people who want to develop their spirituality, explore the many dimensions of existence, and make their dreams come true in physical reality. The essence of grounding isn't a simple matter of being organized, functioning well in the mundane areas of life, or a question of how close one's feet are to the earth. To be grounded entails drawing on the energies of both the material and the spiritual dimensions.

Other Angel info!

Involve your Angels in all that you do! It is not essential that you know the specific Angel to ask to help with specific tasks as the right Angel for that particular job or situation will appear when needed, so remember to use the Angels how they were meant to be used, as our heavenly helpers and messengers.

When you buy a gift for someone, instead of just wrapping it and putting a ordinary card or not with it. Why not get some bright coloured card or glitter sheets and cut up some Angelic symbols or shapes like, wings, for example. These are basic shapes and easy to do, you can then place these cut out in with the gift or in an envelope, and watch how they bring out the inner child as well as a smile in the person that they are meant for, not to mention all those that are around as the recipient opens their gift! This I am sure will be greatly appreciated and will add an extra dimension to your gift.

Ever been stuck for a solution to a problem that you have been trying to solve? Well try this, say to your Angel "if it is for my highest good, please give me an answer or a message or indication to where I can find the answer in the next song that plays on the radio", or you could try saying something similar for the television,

You can also try the following, next time you are driving into town, where you know that there is usually a problem parking, call your angels, and say " please angels, direct me to the ideal parking spot for me this trip, and allow that parking spot to be free for me to park in"

When you have a problem or difficult choice to make, and you are really struggling with it, before you go to sleep at night, call to your Angels, explain to them the problem and ask for them to put the correct choice in your head via a dream by the next morning, then go to sleep and relax in the knowledge that your Angels will put that choice in your mind or dreams while you sleep.

Chapter 3
Walking with Archangels

The Fallen Angels

I was very excited about writing this part of my book as it has always fascinated me, now I know that to some, it may seem a bit odd to include in an Angelic Karma book a section on the fallen ones, but if you really look into it, you will see that it is not so odd, as after all, think of all that they have done, they have got to have some Karmic balancing to do, it will also help to explain to you, that Angelic beings can be just like us, or are we just like them ? I also know that a lot of people are very interested in this subject and the events that took place. I also wanted to include this chapter so that we can all pay tribute to those majestic beings of light that fought and won the Heaven's War. And let's face it, in order to fully understand "white" you must first know "black".

he Fallen Host

These are angels that have fallen from God's grace. Although rarely mentioned these beings serve as a warning to what the wrath of God can bring. Angelologists have a certain interest in these creatures because they have quite an air of shadowy mystery which surrounds them. Fallen angels can be split into two main groups namely, The angels who sided and allied with **Lucifer** during the war in Heaven and the fallen **Watchers** or **Grigori**.

In both of these cases the angels tuned on God, their creator, by misusing the *free will* that had been granted to them by God.

The War in Heaven

There is a general belief that at some point Lucifer joined forces with a third of the divine host in an attempt to place themselves as rulers in the Kingdom of Heaven, by overthrowing God and the faithful angels.

One theory about the cause of the conflict is that when God created man he called upon all of angelic forces to bow before his new creation. Lucifer at that time being one of the highest Archangels found this too humbling by far and refused to debase himself in this manner and duly asked if *"a son of fire should be forced to bow before a son of clay?"*. A similar theory and one very much like the latter suggests that Lucifer should bow before Jesus the son of man. Whatever the reason for the conflict Lucifer appeared to be outgrowing his post as highest of the Seraphim and chief of Angels. It somewhat unclear how many angels were actually engaged in the war in Heaven and the exact number of the host open to conjuncture for many. In the 15th century though it was estimated that 133,306,668 angels fell from the Heavens in a total of 9 days according to the Bishop of Tusculum (c. 1273), and this was reaffirmed by Alphonso de Spina (c. 1460). This number may seem very large, however I was not surprised by the number of fallen angels, when I came upon it, I had thought that this figure would be large, simply due to the fact that it is reported that the number of Angels is extremely large, and seeing as one third of them fell,

Lucifer

The name "Lucifer" means "Light Giver" or "Light Bearer".

Light giver referring to the morning or evening star, Venus. Actually the name meant to mean the "Brightest Star".

That later was translated to "Eosphorus" (Greek word for Morning Star) and finally to Lucifer. In mythology he is the son of Aurora (the Roman personification of dawn) and the father Ceyx (Greek). Contrary to popular belief, Satan and Lucifer are two separate fallen angels. His banishment was because of his complete egotism and pure malice -- his sin, pride. This then indicates that Lucifer, not Satan was indeed the first angel to have sinned. Lucifer has been equated to Satan due to the misreading of the passage Isaiah 14:12 that was applied to the King of Babylon The First concept of this passage is that is was a mention to a man, a king who ruled the city of Babylon on that time.

The second concept is that it was also a reference to Samael, a cosmic being and the Seraphim of Purity, who descended from Heaven to oversee Hell.

Lucifer was a "great" Archangel, Prince, and the anointed Cherub Even after his fall he still seems to retain some of his power and ancient title. There are many different variations of stories and legends on Lucifer.

WHO IS HE?

Is Lucifer the opposite of God? Lucifer cannot be God's opposite because he was created by God.

Lucifer is the opposite of Michael. (the Head Archangel)

Satan

Satan's name is believed to originate from the term *Satan* which connotes the idea of opposition and adversary.

Before his fall, it's believed that he was one of the Ruling Prince's of the Celestial Orders (specifically Seraphim, Cherubim, Powers, and Archangels), chief of the Seraphim and Head of the Order of Virtues.

St. Thomas Aquinas had a different important point on this matter, he believed that Satan was a Cherubim more than anything else Instead of being depicted as a six winged Seraphim, and he was shown as having twelve wings. It has also been written by theologians that Satan was created on the 6th day of Creation. Representing more of an abstract entity than an evil one. He was in charge of testing "humans integrity", though God had the power to set limits on what Satan could and could not do. The traditional theory is that Satan was the angel that betrayed and then led the revolt against God. It boils down to Satan that he was very jealous of the love that God felt towards Adam. Either by transforming into a snake or just using the snake as a tool, Satan tempted Eve with the fruit of the Tree of Knowledge. By 3rd century A.D. it was fully established by the Christian philosopher Origenis the association between the snake and Satan. In following centuries, the snake has been believed to be the incarnation of Satan. God then banished Satan from the Heavens... or did he? He banished him to Earth, but the working theory is that Hell is actually located within the Northern boundaries of the 3rd Heaven. Within the 2nd Heaven the fallen angels are imprisoned awaiting final judgment in complete darkness.

So it's here that Satan walks between Heaven and Earth. Primary staying here on Earth, seeking to destroy the lives of human beings and to keep them separated from God. Here is when Satan is now known by his other name, the Devil.

The Sin

Any rational creature that is, a creature with intellect and will can sin. While angels were yet unbeatified they could sin. And some of them did sin. The sinning angels (or demons) are guilty of all sins in so far as they lead man to commit every kind of sin. But in the bad angels themselves there could be no tendency to fleshly sins, but only to such sins as can be committed by a purely spiritual being, and these sins are two only: pride and envy. Lucifer who latter was confused with his follower Satan, leader of the fallen angels, wished to be as God. This prideful desire was not a wish to be equal to God, for Satan knew by his natural knowledge that equality of creature with creator is utterly impossible. Besides, no creature actually desires to destroy itself, even to become something greater.

On this point man sometimes deceives himself by a trick of imagination; he imagines himself to be another and greater being, and yet it is himself that is somehow this other being. But an angel has no sense-faculty of imagination to abuse in this fashion.

The angelic intellect, with its clear knowledge, makes such self-deception impossible. Lucifer knew that to be equal with God, he would have to be God, and he knew perfectly that this could not be. What he wanted was to be as God; he wished to be like God in a way not suited to his nature, such as to create things by his own power, or to achieve final beatitude without God's help, or to have command over others in a way proper to God alone. Every nature, that is every essence as operating, tends to some good. An intellectual nature tends to good in general, good under its common aspects, good as such. The fallen angels therefore are not naturally evil. The devil did not sin in the very instant of his creation. When a perfect cause makes a nature, the first operation of that nature must be in line with the perfection of its cause. Hence the devil was not created in wickedness. He, like all the angels, was created in the state of sanctifying grace. But the devil, with his companions, sinned immediately after creation. He rejected the grace in which he was created, and which he was meant to use, as the good angels used it, to merit beatitude. If, however, the angels were not created in grace (as some hold) but had grace available as soon as they were created, then it may be that some interval occurred between the creation and the sin of Lucifer and his companions. Lucifer, chief of the sinning angels, was probably the highest of all the angels. But there are some who think that Lucifer was highest only among the rebel angels. The sin of the highest angel was a bad example which attracted the other rebel angels, and, to this extent, was the cause of their sin. The faithful angels are a greater multitude than the fallen angels. For sin is contrary to the natural order. Now, what is opposed to the natural order occurs less frequently, or in fewer instances, than what accords with the natural order.

THE ARCHANGELS

What are Archangels

Archangels are superior or higher-ranking angels, in medieval angelology archangels belonged to the eighth of the nine ranks of the Celestial Hierarchy The word from Middle English and from Old

French is 'archangele' and 'archangelus' from Late Latin. 'Arkhangelos' from Late Greek.

The Archangels are the captains of all the angelic hosts, having been created as the foremost hierarchs in the angelic kingdom. They are majestic beings who personify divine attributes and are at the service of the mankind of earth. They work tirelessly to defeat evil and promote good. The Archangels have divine complements or twin flames, just as people do. The Archangels predate us by millions of years and it has been said that they were our first teachers on the spiritual path. They have also been described as divine architects, whom God uses to draft and execute the plans for his projects. They are cosmic builders and designers in the grandest sense of the word, arcing to our minds the divine blueprint for every endeavour, from the smallest to the greatest. All of the Archangels are also healers who are masters at healing our souls. Imagine the power of the Archangels, who for millions of years have done nothing but affirm the reality of God and expand spiritual light in their being. Then when they are in our midst, they minister to us and purify us by transmitting the immense increments of light that they have garnered. Using this boost of energy from the angels properly can help us make much greater progress in our daily life and on the spiritual path.

There are four main Archangels that watch over us, Michael, Raphael, Gabriel and Uriel. Other Archangels that I work with are Jophiel, Chamuel and Zadkiel

Angels are neither male nor female although sometimes the female element may have another name such as Uriel and Ariel. Although there is much written about the Archangels, the elements that they govern and what they are most known for, and much of this differs, but the information that I will give you in this chapter is how I see them and how I work with them, some of you will see them differently, so experience the energy of each archangel as see what feels right for you.

Archangels are able to be in many places at one time. You never have to feel that your "problem" isn't important enough to bother them with. That is what they're there for, to help you grow Remember when you make your requests to an archangel, they are not able to interfere with your karma.

Lianne Lockyer

Archangel Sandalphon

Sandalphon's name means 'brother' in Greek, a reference to his twin brother, the archangel Metatron. The twins are the only archangels in heaven who were originally mortal men. Sandalphon's chief role is to carry human prayers to God, so they may be answered. Archangel Sandolphon is connected to the earth energies, he will remind you of the importance of being grounded, he will help you to establish a secure link between heaven and earth .Sandaphon is very aware that it is sometimes difficult to be in the physical world, yet it is an experience that we ourselves have chosen, and that we are privileged to be here at this time.

Sandalphon is the Guardian angel over the Earth Kingdom and patron angel of music and Heavenly song. He is responsible for bringing the original blueprint of humanity and all beings in the physical world into existence and so can also act as guide, helping steer you in the right direction. He also decides on the gender of an embryo.

Sandalphon is considered to be the tallest of angels, being described as over 500 years tall. Mosses once referred to him as the 'tall angel' and was filled with fear at his appearance. It has been said it would take a five-hundred year journey to travel from this feet to his head. Other reports describe him as being of fiery appearance, or made of pure energy, difficult to gaze upon.

Sandalphon is believed to have been an angelic prince. He was originally Elijah, the prophet of Israel. It is said that he was carried to heaven in a burning chariot by a whirlwind, while still alive. It was at this point that he became Sandolphon. As Sandalphon he holds a position in the angelic hierarchy behind Merkabah - the heavenly chariot.

Archangel Sandalphon can bring gentleness into all areas of your life. He can help you be kind and gentle, yet powerful. His stone is turquoise, which can slow your heart rate and breathing. One of Sandalphon's principal roles is to help answer our prayers. He can help you allow yourself to receive. He can help you live with integrity, bring spiritual gifts of prophecy, allow healing, and support manifestation. Sandalphon can help you speak the truth.

Related Colour	Red, Brown, Green
Related Chakra	1st Base
Related Emotional Issues courage, patience	Survival, support,
Related Health Issues bowels, Kidneys,	Lower Digestive Tract,
	Spinal column, legs, bones

Archangel Jophiel

Jophiel is the 'Angel of Paradise and Illumination'. Jophiel heals negative situations and brings beauty and organization into our lives. He is associated with anything beautiful, and can help us see the beauty both without and within, and can help rid feelings of jealously. If you need more sharpness of mind for passing exams, inspiration for projects at work or an understanding of how to resolve a conflict, you can ask Jophiel for help he can also rescue people from ignorance or spiritual blindness that might keep them from fulfilling their souls' highest potential.

There is not much written in traditional lore about Archangel Jophiel. He is known as the angel of beauty, for his name in Hebrew translates to "beauty of God." It is generally believed that Jophiel drove Adam and Eve from the Garden of Eden. Not surprisingly, Jophiel guarded the Tree of Knowledge, which played a crucial role in their expulsion from paradise. The metaphor for the beginning of the separation of man's thought from the divine was when Eve tasted the fruit of knowledge, thus breaking the "at-one-ment" with God. When Eve bit into the apple she began to perceive both evil and good. The introduction of evil led mankind to forget what absolute truth was. Everything would become relative, and man could no longer distinguish absolute goodness from the good that is only good in comparison to evil. So the mission of these twin flames is to illuminate mankind with understanding of the teachings of Christ, Mohammed, and all the other prophets and angels. The flames represent the phrase "I AM Light," which is a feeling that descends upon enlightened souls. Jesus said, "I am the way, the truth, and the light." In other words, he is saying "the wisdom that I bring you is God's wisdom and I bring it to you to use in your life."

Whenever there is a spark of inspiration toward spiritual growth, the angels of illumination are brought in to magnetize that fusion.

Jophiel also wishes to bestow on you great light and joy, he wants to bring fun and laughter into your life. Do not spend all your time working, relax and enjoy life, whenever you feel down and fed up, Jophiel reminds you that he is here to light up your life.

Call Jophiel if you wish to experience flashes of insight and clarity,

His aura is deep rose pink

Colour	Yellow
Related Chakra	3rd Solar Plexus, 6th third eye.
Related emotional issues self esteem, emotional	personal power, confidence, low
	Stability.
Related health issues and heartburn, control	Upper Digestive tract, indigestion
	Food intake.

Archangel Uriel

Some accounts place the Archangel Uriel at the head of the third order or company of angels. Others identify Uriel as one of the Seven Spirits before the Throne. Archangel Uriel has been called "the Lord of powerful action" Uriel personifies the Divine Fire that comes down from the Third Aspect of Deity--Universal Mind--penetrating each plane until It reaches the physical. There, the Fire ignites the fusion in the centre of the Sun, the fission at the centre of the Earth, and the kundalini at the base of the spine. It creates worlds, universes, and life--which then await the quickening impulse of the Second Aspect to evolve and grow.

The ***Book of Enoch*** describes Uriel as "one of the holy angels, who is over the world... the leader of them all." Later we read in the same book: "Uriel showed to me, whom the Lord of glory hath set for ever over all the luminaries of the heaven... the sun, moon, and stars, all the ministering creatures which make their revolution in all the chariots of the heaven."

The name Uriel translates to "light of God" ask him to illuminate a situation or relationship that is bringing you anxiety or confusion , and you will gain new clarity and insight into which direction to take, Uriel aura is a beautiful pale yellow, the colour of spiritual growth,

Uriel helps with the release of resentment, anger and unforgivness. He teaches us that these thoughts and feelings are really only harmful to us, and that when we decide to willingly let them go, we free, not only the person whom these thoughts and feelings were directed at, but ourselves also.

Uriel brings you the qualities of peace through determination and transmutation. He is here to help you deal with your inner conflicts,

Related Colour	Gold and Purple
Related Chakra	1st base and 3rd Solar Plexus
Related Emotional Issues courage, Emotional	Personal Power, Confidence,
	Stability
Related Health Issues	Upper Digestive Tract, Control of Insulin, And addictions

Archangel Raphael

The Angel of healing, whose name means "God Heals" Raphael is charged with the healing of our beloved, He begins with purifying our minds and erasing false beliefs.

It's sensible for everyone to call upon Archangel Raphael for his help in healing.

Ask Raphael for help when you are in any kind of pain, whether it is physical, emotional romantic, intellectual or spiritual. He will somehow inspire you with sudden ideas and thoughts giving you just the right information to help the healing. Pay attention to and then follow these angelic answers to your prayers.

When asked for healing assistance, Raphael surrounds and nurtures people with the emerald green light of his halo. Green is the colour of healing and clairvoyant people may see emerald green sparkles when Raphael is around.

Except for situations where the person's death or illness is part of their overall divine plan, Archangel Raphael will energetically supply whatever is needed to promote healing. It's important to note He will not always swoop in and heal everything right away. He could let you know that your negative thoughts have created this illness and to get rid of it, you must change your thinking. Hand over old anger to him for cleansing in the light. When this anger is gone, you will feel much more at peace and the effects of rage and anger in your body can be healed.

Raphael coaches and motivates healers whispering instructions into the ears of doctors, surgeons, psychologists, nurses and other caregivers including scientists. His intervention helps scientists in making breakthroughs in medical cures.

Ask for Raphael's participation to promote healing in rocky marriages, addiction, grief and loss, family relationships and stressful lifestyles. Simply say his name or make a specific request: "Archangel Raphael, please come to my side and help me feel better about [issue]. Please surround me in your healing energy and guide my actions and thoughts so that I am healed."

Raphael is also the archangel in charge of travel. As you check in at the airport, ask Raphael watch over your luggage, the plane and your travels. Raphael and the traveller angels and can control airplane turbulence, give you directions when you're lost, keep a leaky tire inflated and prevent your car from running out of petrol (for a while anyway!).

If Archangel Raphael were to come to you, then this would indicate that you are a natural healer, your friends would more than likely come to you with their problems

Related Colour	Green , Deep Pink
Related Chakra	4th Heart

Archangel Chamuel

When you've problems, which relate to matters of the heart, then Archangel Chamuel is the angel you call upon in your hour of need. Archangel Chamuel works alongside you and helps your heart to heal. If you've been hurt, and you're suffering from a broken heart, then by calling upon Archangel Chamuel and asking him for assistance you'll find the divine energy to help you mend your broken heart. Archangel Chamuel's name means "He who seeks God".

Archangel Chamuel will assist you with Love. Finding lost possessions. Substance abuse. Artistic expression. Finding accommodation. World peace.

This Angel of unconditional love lifts you from your sorrow, helping you to love yourself and others, to express your inner feelings, and to release your negative emotions and thus mending your bruised and battered heart. If there's a breakdown of your relationship, if you cling to your relationships and don't allow your companion the freedom to be able to express themselves freely, call on Chamuel for guidance and support. The other areas you can Chamuel can help is if you need to strengthen a parent-child bond, if you're unable to feel love for yourself or others, if your heart has hardened and is full of negative emotions, if you have lost someone close through death or separation, if you and your children have experienced a divorce, if your heart is blocked with depression, hopelessness and despair, if you feel lonely and broken hearted, if you need to be loved, if you are judgmental and cynical or if you don't appreciate the love that you have in your life.

Related Colour	Magenta Pink
Related Chakra	4th Heart and 2nd Chakra
Related Emotional Issues	To give and receive unconditional love. Forgiveness
	Emotional Stability, to find strength in Vulnerability
Related Health Issues	Heart and Vascular Disease, lungs, arms, Hands
	Immune System, Allergies, Cancer M.E , A.I.D.S

Archangel Gabriel

The Archangel Gabriel is the exalted Messenger of God, whose name means "The Strength of God" Because of Gabriel's role as a communicator and mediator between Heaven and Earth, Catholics hold the Archangel to be a Patron Saint of broadcasters, telecommunications workers, diplomats, messengers, postal workers, and stamp collectors. Because Gabriel helped the prophet Daniel interpret his dreams, those seeking similar aid with their own dream work may call on Archangel Gabriel for help. Additionally, because Gabriel announced the births of both John the Baptist and Jesus Christ, women hoping for heavenly assistance in trying to conceive children have reported benefits from keeping an Angel Gabriel novena candle burning in the home. Archangel Gabriel's dominant theme is angelic joy. Gabriel's nature is one of pure joy…and, as such, he has long provided humanity with ongoing support as we all search for and often struggle with the creation of joy in our lives. He offers you, inspiration and divine inner strength during times of great challenge…those times when there appears to be little to be joyful about. He is especially able to help you with inner communications for accessing your 'knowing' and 'intuition,' as well as provide practical support for effective communications in your outer, day-to-day life. In his role as communicator, Gabriel also serves as the announcer and harbinger of good news and information. It is no accident that Gabriel is coming forward to offer his support and energies in the form of his Angel Link. At this particular time, he is heralding in special new energies that are beginning to flow into our global-human energy system...to ultimately prepare us all for our next spiritual evolutionary leap.

The Angels purpose is to do the will of God. Archangel Gabriel is a teacher and a messenger of truth. He has historically provided Leadership.

Gabriel can help you fearlessly tap in to this power. Archangel Gabriel reassures you that it is safe for you to be powerful, and protects you in all way. Gabriel's aura is copper. When you wear the crystal stone citrine, or the precious metal copper, you readily connect with Archangel Gabriel's energy.

Related Chakra	Sacral (2nd)
Related Colour:	Peach
Related Emotional Issues:	Emotional balance
Crystals:	Citrine, Carnelian, Golden topaz
Life Lesson:	Challenging motivations based on social conditioning

Archangel Michael

Archangel Michael is referred to as the greatest of all angels in writings throughout the world, including Jewish, Christian and Islamic Michael the Archangel involves himself closely with the Earth and its inhabitants, , especially now in order to bring the cleansing, reforming power of **Light** and **Truth** so that the old beliefs in materialism, greed, self, conflict and possession may be seen for the illusions that they are, and may be replaced with joy, peace, hope, compassion, tolerance, understanding and **Love**.

Michael has been, and is, seen in many forms, often associated with wings of streaming brightness, depth and colour, and classical armour, bearing his sword of truth. All those who hear or see him or feel his presence describe his uniqueness, identifiably and strength always feeling comforted empowered and befriended in the experience.

Michael is often regarded as God's most senior Archangel, working in close harmony with his fellow Archangels, and overseeing the angels who "are without number", supporting them in their dedicated roles and offering a presence of strength and will when extra help is needed. Above all, Michael reminds us that we are each of us perfect children of God, that every being can overcome darkness with the great armoury of truth and endless Love, and that the experience of the Earth is less a trial of discovery or learning more our opportunity for emergence, for expression of the God - self, in the process of return to the source of all perfection and grace.

You can ask Michael to cut any ties that bind you to others, or negative emotions, past, present or past life to help you to let go and move on (we will be explain the method of this later in the book) .

Michael gives us the strength to face any obstacle, no matter how insurmountable it may seem. Just ask him to give you the strength and courage to face the future, whatever is happening in your life,

Related Colour:	Blue, Topaz yellow
Related Emotional Issues: protection	Truth, courage, Strength,
Crystals:	Blue lace agate, blue calcite, tiger's eye, lapis lazuli
Related Chakra:	Throat, Solar Plexus

Archangel Zadkiel

Archangel Zadkiel (Zedekiel) was known as the benevolent and merciful Chief of the Order of Dominions, the Hashmallim, who were fiery foundational righteousness angels. In the *Zohar*, Archangel Zadkiel was mentioned as the standard bearer of Archangel Michael during conflicts. A *Keeper of Righteous Memories*, he was also a Chieftain of the flaming revelations Shinanim.

His name means 'Righteousness of God'

He is working on the seventh ray (violet) of transmutation.

Archangel Zadkiel works on the silver ray of mercy and grace and is associated with the violet flame of transmutation, which is under the guardianship of Saint Germaine. They can both be invoked to surround a person or situation with the silver violet flame of Transmutation and Mercy. This is one of the most powerful transmutation tools available to humanity at this time. He helps people find forgiveness, diplomacy and tolerance

Archangel Zadkiel works with the Soul Star chakra – 6 inches above the top of our heads.

His twin flame is Amethyst.

Zadkiel wishes to remind us of the healing power of forgiveness, He asks you to stop punishing yourself and to release the negativity in your heart and move on.

Call on Zadkiel to help you to strengthen your link with the divine, he can also help you to transmute negative energy into positive energy and to heal traumas from past lives.

Related Colour:	Violet
Related Emotional Issues:	Idealism, Spiritual will, confusion, depression.
Crystals:	Amethyst, Charvoite, Clear quartz, selenite
Related Chakra:	Crown Chakra.

Book 2

Chapter 4
Karma & Reincarnation

What is Karma & Reincarnation?

Have you ever wondered why some people born crippled or blind and others are geniuses?

Why you seem to instantly like or dislike certain people?

Why you find yourself in similar unpleasant situations again and again?

How you end up with a family you have nothing in common with?

Why do some people die as children and others in old age? Well, you're not alone.

The hidden truth behind such statements is "What goes around comes around." This concept of karma is taught by the great lights of both East and West. Although the word "karma" has made it into everyday language that many of us use daily, but few of us really understand what the word really means. But luckily for us, the Angels and Ascended Masters are here to teach us what to do to balance Karma, to transmute negative into positive, to enable us all to reach our full potential both as human beings, as well as to achieve spiritual ascension

Karma is sometimes called the law of the circle. It requires that whatever we do for good or bad returns full circle to our doorstep so that our soul can learn life lessons and gain self-mastery. We determine our own fate by our thoughts, feelings, words and deeds. Our free will choices in the past set the course for our current circumstances, and the choices we make today will determine our future.

The companion law to karma is the law of reincarnation. Reincarnation provides the necessary cycles of time and opportunity our soul needs in order for us to balance our karmic debts, fulfil our divine plan, achieve mastery and bond to our Higher Self. It is simply not possible to accomplish all this in one lifetime.

For as long as History goes back, people have always wondered, if there is life after death, is death really the end of existence?, or is death simply an entry into eternity, or an intermission between earthly lives? Some teach that the soul reincarnates in many different bodies, why are so many of us curious about reincarnation, could it be that Reincarnation offers hope to many. If we don't get it right in this life, we have another chance the next time around. Although, even those of us who believe in reincarnation will tell you that the vast majority of humans do not remember their previous lives. So with this being the case, how then can we learn from our past mistakes if we cannot remember them? We seem to make the same mistakes over and over again.

An angelic force of gravity shapes cosmic order, karma shapes experiential order. Our long sequence of lives is a tapestry of creating and resolving karmas-positive, negative and an amalgam of the two.

Many people are very curious about their past lives and expend great time, effort and money to explore them. Actually, this curious probing into past lives is unnecessary. Indeed it is a natural protection from reliving past trauma or becoming infatuated more with our past lives that our present life that the inner recesses of the muladhara memory chakra are not easily accessed. For, as we exist now is a sum total of all our past lives. In our present moment, our mind and body state is the cumulative result of the entire spectrum of our past lives. So, no matter how great the intellectual knowing of these two key principles, it is how we currently live that positively shapes karma and unfolds us spiritually. Knowing the laws, we are responsible to resolve blossoming karmas from past lives and create karma that, projected into the future, will advance, not hinder, us.

Karma literally means "deed or act," but more broadly describes the principle of cause and effect. Simply stated, karma is the law of action and reaction which governs consciousness. The akashic memory in our higher chakras continuously records the soul's memories during each of its earth lives, and in the astral/mental world's in-between earth existences. Ancient yogis, in psychically studying the time line of cause/effect, assigned three categories to karma. The first is sanchita, the sum total of past karma yet to be resolved. The second category is prarabdha, that portion of sanchita karma being experienced in the present life. Kriyamana, the third type, is karma you are presently creating. However, it must be understood that your past negative karma can be altered into a smoother, easier state through the loving, heart-chakra nature, through dharma and sadhana. That is the key of karmic wisdom. Live religiously well and you will create positive karma for the future and soften negative karma of the past.

Karma operates not only individually, but also in ever-enlarging circles of group karma where we participate in the sum karma of multiple souls. This includes family, community, nation, race and religion, so if we individually or collectively, unconditionally love and give, we will be loved and given to. The individuals or groups who act soulfully or maliciously toward us are the vehicle of our own karmic creation. The people who manifest your karma are also living through past karma and simultaneously creating future karma. For example, if their karmic pattern did not include miserliness, they would not be involved in your karma of selfishness. Another person may express some generosity toward you, fulfilling the gifting karma of your past experience. Imagine how intricately interconnected all the cycles of karma are for our planet's life forms.

Many people believe in the principle of karma, but don't apply its laws to their daily life or even to life's peak experiences. Then they shout out, why is this happened to me? What did I do to deserve this? Whenever anything bad happens to them, they seem to forget that it is us that create our own experiences. It is really an exercising of our soul's powers of creation. Karma, then, is our best spiritual teacher. We spiritually learn and grow as our actions return to us to be resolved and dissolved. In this highest sense, there is no good and bad karma; there is self-created experience that presents opportunities for spiritual advancement. If we can't draw lessons from the karma, then we resist and/or resent it, lashing out with mental, emotional or physical force. The original substance of that karmic event is spent and no longer exists, but the current reaction creates a new condition of harsh karma.

We now know that life doesn't end with the death of the biological body. The soul continues to occupy the astral body, a subtle, luminous duplicate of the physical body. This subtle body is made of higher-energy astral matter and dwells in a dimension called the astral plane. If the soul body itself is highly evolved, it will occupy the astral/mental bodies on a very refined plane of the astral known as the Devaloka, "the world of light-shining beings." At death, the soul slowly becomes totally aware in its astral/mental bodies and it predominantly lives through those bodies in the astral dimension.

The soul functions with complete continuity in its astral/mental bodies. It is with these sensitive vehicles that we experience dream or "astral" worlds during sleep every night. The astral world is equally as solid and beautiful, as varied and comprehensive as the earth dimension- if not much more so. Spiritual growth, psychic development, guidance in matters of governance and commerce, artistic cultivation, inventions and discoveries of medicine, science and technology all continue by astral people who are "in-between" earthly lives. Because certain seed karmas can only be resolved in earth consciousness and because the soul's initial realizations of Absolute Reality are only achieved in a physical body, our soul re-enters a new biological body. At the right time, and so starts another earth life that will best fulfill its karmic pattern.

During our many earth lives, a wide range of life patterns are experienced. We exist as male and female, often switching back and forth from life to life as the nature becomes more harmonized into a person exhibiting both feminine nurturing and masculine intrepidness. We come to earth as rich people, poor people, murderers, religious people, we come back as every race, religion creed and type that you can imagine, and others that you cant! This is so that you can experience everything; learn all that you need to learn, from every point of view...

When we take a hard look around us, the world doesn't seem to make much sense. If we go by appearances, it would seem that countless people have escaped the noose of fate: many an evil person has died peacefully in bed. Worse, good and noble people have suffered without apparent cause, their goodness being repaid by hatred and torture. Witness the Holocaust; witness child abuse.

If we look only on the surface, the universe appears absurd at best, malevolent at worst. But that's because we're not looking deeply; we're only viewing this lifetime, seeing neither the lives that precede this one nor the lives that may follow. When we see a calamity or a triumph, we're seeing only one freeze frame of a very, very long movie. We can see neither the beginning nor the end of the movie. What we do know, however, is that everyone, no matter how depraved, will eventually, through the course of many lifetimes and undoubtedly through much suffering, come to realize his or her own divine nature. That is the inevitable happy ending of the movie.

Life's real attainment is not money, not material luxury, not sexual or eating pleasure, not intellectual, business or political power, or any other of the instinctive or intellectual needs. These are natural pursuits, to be sure, but our divine purpose on this earth is to personally realize our identity in and with God. After many lifetimes of wisely controlling the creation of karma and resolving past karmas when they return, the soul is fully matured in the knowledge of these divine laws and the highest use of them.

How to Balance negative Karma

There are three main ways to balance any negative karma the first way is the most common way however it is also the slowest, which is to simply, live through it. I can understand you all thinking, "come on there must be a better way" and yes there are other ways but however difficult this way may be the best for some , for example, in this life a person may marry and support those who he abandoned or even betrayed in a former life, Or he may have to suffer through the abuse that he had previously doled out to others, this being the case, you can see how the best way to deal with this kind of negative Karma would be to "just live through it " there is no quick fix for this, it has to be lived through in order to balance your negative karma.

The second way to balance your negative Karma is to "tip the scales" doing good deeds, this can be done through selfless service to life, for example, working tirelessly in nursing homes, hospitals, teaching others, charity work, anything where you put yourself out to make the lives of others better. Maybe this is why people who do this kind of selfless work always say " it is hard work, but it just makes me feel better doing it" this is because it is tipping the scales away from the negative and into the positive.

The third and perhaps the fastest way to balance Karma is by using a special gift from the ascended masters, which is called the Silver Violet Flame, as Invoking this high frequency spiritual energy can literally dissolve negative Karmic patterns, and help you gain self-mastery and free you from the rounds of rebirth. We will be going deeper into the Silver Violet flame in the next section.

Actions that can generate negative Karma includes the following -

Killing including animals, unless that murder was as a result of self defence.

Theft.

Intentionally hurting someone in any way.

Causing someone else to suffer in any way,

resenting someone; your anger may cause you to be confronted with similar circumstances in the future

Not taking responsibility for yourself, or for your part in any conflict.

Being unable to forgive.

addiction, if it hurts you or anyone around you

disrespecting yourself to the point of personal harm (such as being a martyr); yes you can gain good karma by helping others through martyrdom, but you still may have to balance

a lack of self-respect

Telling a lie that hurts someone else in any way, even if you are not caught and even if you believe your own lie

Some situations that are often believed to produce negative karma, but do not, include the following:

making or earning a lot of money honestly.

If you have a lot of money yet do not give away a lot to charities does not produce negative Karma, the world is not your responsibility, of course if you do you gain karmic credits or in some cases, pay back karmic debts by helping others, and it feels good!

Lying to protect someone, as long as you're not hurting another person in the process, or if helping that person means that you are assisting them to dodge taking responsibility for their actions.

Breaking up with a partner, as long as you are not intentionally doing anything to hurt them in the process; their resistance and difficulty with it is not your responsibility.

Divorce, as long as you take care of your responsibilities and leave peacefully.

Sex before Marriage, as long as it does not hurt anyone else, including you.

Unfaithfulness.

Accidentally hurting someone in any way, but any guilt could cause you to experience a reaction in the future if you don't let go of it.

Homosexuality

prostitution, as long as it's between two consenting adults.

Being a single parent or having a child outside of marriage, as long as you provide for the child and be the best parent you can be.

Also just to let you know, confessing your sins to, say a priest, or during prayer. Will not get you out of any negative Karma that you may have created. It is wise to bear in mind that no-one, however spiritual they are can cheat Karma or avoid any future negative Karma. Everyone will need to return to base camp (earth in future lives) until all their Karma is balanced and paid back. Basically anyone who "does not do the right thing in any given situation" is essentially buying a return trip back to this planet for another life to endure another lifetime of tests once again. OK, I would be the first to admit that "doing the right thing" is sometimes all but impossible due to the forces of personal fate, as the majority of people, more often than not, will only act or behave in accordance with their personal knowledge and awareness, rather than the way they "could or should" if they wanted to reduce the level of Karmic consequences, But maybe learning from this and learning the way to "do the right thing" is one of our tests? In any case at least you know that ultimately it is up to us personally as to the level of negative Karma we accumulate or pay back. In other words, what happens to us after death and what happens during any future lifetime is in our hands, we only have ourselves to blame or indeed thank!

I have been asked so many times "why would I have chosen such a bad life? Why would I have chosen to suffer so much? Something must be wrong," in these cases

It is worth remembering that even when things seem really bad for you personally here on earth, and you may be dreading the next day, although I can totally understand that it is no comfort to be told "hey its your fault, you chose this life!" whereas on a soul level you may understand the more spiritual reasons for why you're here and why you may be suffering, on a physical level you just can not fathom it out, but sometimes you are not supposed to know the bigger picture before the time is right, as they may well be additional lessons to be learnt in the process, that may not be learnt if you were fully aware of the situation . But as you become more aware of yourself and your life, you will find that you start perceiving the deeper reasons for your life journey.

According to research involving past life regression, souls can decide to stay "on the other side" instead of return for another life, this is particularly if in previous lifetimes they have managed to work through al of their Karma, or they can decide to learn their life lessons in different ways they may even decide to stay on the other side and help those of us here on earth .Most people cannot fully remember if they've been here enough already, or where they are in regards to Karmic Balance, but some with very strong psychic and Mediumship abilities may receive strong impressions that this may be one of the last ones. Of course, many people say this is their last lifetime, but how do they really know that? Perhaps they feel they are a very old soul, but that could just mean they took many lifetimes to get where they are today, not that they have balanced all necessary karma. Or maybe they may feel they're ready to move beyond earth, and that they're spiritually aware enough to break the cycle of reincarnation. But in saying that The best way to make sure you finish your lifetimes here on earth as quickly as possible and, eventually, enjoy more of the good things in life, is to "do the right thing" from now on, in every situation.

The Silver Violet Flame

One of the keys to changing past karma and fulfilling your divine mission with your twin flame is the violet flame - a unique spiritual energy that has the power to literally erase the negative karma that keeps you from your twin flame and God. While you can't go back in time, the violet flame has the power to erase, or transmute the cause, the effect, and even the memory of our past mistakes. Transmutation means to change - to alter in form, appearance or nature. The violet flame changes negative energy into positive energy, darkness into light, "fate" into opportunity. The flame also erases the resultant "bad karma" of our mistakes. Our past actions - both good and bad - do come back to us. This is the law of karma. This impersonal cosmic law decrees that whatever we do comes full circle to our doorstep for resolution; simply, what goes around comes around.

In general, most people must pay their debt to life, or "balance" their karma, by selflessly reaching out and helping others, by working through misfortunes that come their way, or by passing through diseases or other forms of personal suffering. But it need not be so with the violet flame! The violet flame is able to transmute or mitigate our negative karma before it comes back to us.

On the physical level, the violet flame can help heal our bodies by removing the karma that makes us vulnerable to illness and disease. But the real cause of disease is often rooted in our mental, emotional and spiritual states.

The Violet Flame transmutes energies allowing a soul to burn off the karmic ties that bind it to the emotional grid or physical realms. Its purpose is to transmute negative energy into positive energy. The flame is a tool to help you release karma, raise frequency and consciousness awareness, accelerate spiritual growth, to activate your DNA. The violet flame can also help you deal with emotional and psychological problems to some degree. If you believe in its power, it can help relieve stress, depression and anger.

How the Violet Flame Works

The violet flame works by changing "vibrations". In physics, vibration is the speed of oscillation - the speed at which something moves back and forth. On the atomic level, vibration can be understood to be the speed at which electrons orbit around the nucleus of the atom. The violet flame works by changing vibrations on this level. Atoms are mostly empty space. The empty space between the nucleus and the electrons is where negative energy and karma can become stuck. When the atoms in our bodies and auras become clogged with this negativity, the electrons whirl slower and slower, and we begin to resonate more with negativity and less with light - we have a lower vibration, and become less spiritual. The violet flame transmutes this negative energy. It does not simply surround and remove the energy, but transforms it into light. Because there is less density within the atom, the electrons whirl faster and faster, thereby raising your vibration.

When you have a higher vibration, there is more spiritual energy in your body. Acupuncturists and yogis know that optimum health comes when this spiritual energy flows freely throughout the body. The violet flame frees up this energy and re-establishes harmony and equilibrium, propelling you into a more spiritual state of being.

The violet flame is linked to Saint Germain, indeed it was given to us from Saint Germain and during the process of being attuned to the flame Saint Germain is present. When the violet flame is invoked you may see or sense heat from the violet flame. To those who have been attuned or have developed their spiritual sight, the violet flame appears as a physical violet fire. You may also be able to "see" the violet flame at work with your inner eye, by concentrating on the spiritual centre between your eyebrows.

You can also use the violet flame to help family and friends. Just visualize the violet flame around them.

Even a few minutes of visualising and invoking the violet flame will produce results, but persistence is needed to penetrate age-old habits you would like to change. You can start out with just a few minutes of violet flame in the morning to help you through the day, and you can add the violet flame to whatever prayers or meditations you currently practice.

Calling forth the violet flame daily is one of the quickest and most effective means for accelerating spiritual growth in preparation for our ultimate reunion with God and our twin flame. The only true and lasting union of twin flames is for each of you first, together or separately, to achieve union with God. Then you, your twin flame and God are united and inseparable forevermore.

Karmic Relationships

Karmic relationships can appear to be very confusing, and there are many types of "Karmic relationships" but in a nut shell Karmic relationships involve two people who are drawn together for the balancing of mutual Karmic Debts. These relationships are quite often, as you would expect hard work and can be very difficult, however they are particularly important for the purpose of making progress on your spiritual path. It is worth noting though that we can be in a Karmic relationship with anyone, Karmic relationships are not exclusive to love relationships, it can also be with a best friend, brother, sister, the postman, your mum, anyone.

If the Karmic relationship involves the individuals marrying then, the couple can make good karma for bringing forth and nurturing children. Some of these marriages may provide opportunity for balancing the more serious karmas such as murder, betrayal or extreme hatred and resentment from a previous lifetime. Very often the only way we can balance these serious karmas is by the love expressed through the husband and wife relationship. These relationships can often begin with the most intense love or desire, which early on can be mistaken for the twin flame relationship. Which we will go into in depth at a later stage

Sometimes we will get together with someone in order to balance old debts. This is very common and can sometimes be misleading. That occurs when we believe that this is a lifetime relationship but it is actually intended to last only long enough to even an old score. I suspect that this is what happens sometimes in marriages when one partner supports another through an educational phase and then the educated partner leaves. Perhaps this was a pay-back of support given in the other direction in the past.

If you are in a Karmic relationship, it may be worth noting that the relationship often ends once the debt is paid, or when spirit decides that the time of opportunity is up. So it may be important to ask, how would you know if you are in a Karmic relationship? As no relationship is perfect right? Correct, but there is a sure fire way of telling, for instance, do you feel you need some kind of therapy as a result of being with this person? If so this could be an indicator, as are feeling drained emotionally, physically and even financially, are you doing all the giving whereas your partner is just take, take, take ? These are all indicators of a Karmic relationship.

The thought of having Karma of any kind in a relationship is kind of freaky, no matter how it is showing itself. There can be the feeling that you "know" your partner before you have really got to know them, of knowing what makes them tick. Although this can be a positive feeling which can, deepen the emotions and making you far more aware of their actions and behaviour than you might normally have been. It can also be a negative feeling, in which the couple involve seem to be reliving bad behaviour patterns which can involve abuse, neglect and such like, Some long-term abuse situations appear to be old habit patterns in action, a "We've always done this," sort of condition. This behaviour is from their past lives, and they are acting it out as if it were a film loop, running over and over the same material. They are doing this instead of putting thing right and balancing out their Karma. Nasty karmic situations can often be marked by violence or tragedy.

Many "Karma aware" people may feel that it would be a good idea to make their decisions about relationships based upon the Karma that it carries, but this will cause many to avoid their life lessons, as the relationships they avoid was most likely to have been placed there to teach them a valuable life lesson, or karmic balance. This does appear to be part of the consequence of running a more "Karma aware" relationship. The lessons that we have to learn from each other can be as varied as life itself. One thing is certain however, that the lesson is a deep and personal one and left to our own devices, we would probably do everything possible to avoid. This may be why such spiritual devices are part of our lives, to provide an external force to motivate the learning experience. Karmic relationships are valuable gifts that can help us on our spiritual journey. This can only occur however, if we're willing to let go of the petty ego structures that we find useful as one-lifetime-only propositions. When we can take our entire spiritual existence into account and act from that perspective, major learning experiences can take place.

Breaking out of a karmic pattern can be constructive whether the love relationship is having trouble or not. The good thing is that just deciding that you want to make the choice to work out relationship karma; we are demonstrating our readiness to be free of it. Some ways of making this work are to acknowledge your own repetitive behaviour, have you found yourself saying or thinking, "I always attract the bad ones" "why does everyone I have a relationship with always treat me like that" if this is you, then just think about that repetitive behaviour, It is safe to assume that we continue to be drawn to the same person or types or person in order to share learning and assist in each other's evolutionary process. The best thing to do in those situations seems to be trying to avoid acting out the same experiences and instead, develop new approaches and solutions to life. I know that it is can seem to be far easier though to continue acting from, time-worn habits of behaviour, some of which may seem "right" simply because we've done them so often. These can include being the punching bag for the partner who has never been motivated to find a different expression for his/her anger, or being the "bad guy" for the martyr who has developed no other focus for self-esteem. Our job in the relationship is to provide an evolutionary impetus for each other to find the new solutions and not play out roles which are damaging to ourselves and our partners. Once acknowledged and understood, you are demonstrating that you are learning that lesson and you will be able to move on from that, equally when we are in a punishment or debt-oriented cycle with a specific partner, we can choose to work together as equals to end the old competitive pattern. We can set aside our need to be right or controlling and find ways to support one another.

Becoming more aware of karmic situations is so very rewarding, its literally retaking control of our lives, our spiritual debts, mental patterns and personality quirks are things that we can move through and consequently transform. This is our evolutionary destiny and we can influence it. So don't worry and think that all karmic love relationships have to be painful and difficult. As you choose to be more Karmic aware you can transform negative patterns by choosing to be free from it.

Karmic Marriage

Whether it is the union of twin flames, soul mates or karmic partners, the marriage of man and woman is meant to be an initiation on the path back to God, a commemoration of the soul's reunion with God. It is our choice as to whether our relationships are based on the human or the divine. The union of twin flames is intended to be for the magnification of their service to God and humanity - it is a high and holy calling. To meet your twin flame while you still have karma may simply lead to another parting, without the knowledge of spiritual laws on how to balance this karma and the dedication to apply these laws. Here, the two individuals are drawn together for the balancing of mutual karma. As mentioned in the previous chapter these marriages are often difficult but they are important in achieving mastery on the Path. The husband and wife also gain the good karma of sponsoring and nurturing their children.

I have always believed that when you marry you also take on each others Karma. And that I believe is the real meaning of the vows you take "in sickness and in health" to me means "in cycles of Karma" So that is the seriousness of a marriage vow. And this is why some people may resist marriage. This is also the reasoning behind the phrase "The honeymoon is over" basically when you are deciding upon something as serious you have to ask "Do I want to share in that person's karma?" And karma is circumstance. And the type of person that person is and the problems they have or the things they get into, even their career, is their karma.

We may meet people in life to whom we have been married in previous lives. Our karmic ties and our deep emotional ties and our unresolved relationships all usually cross our path in a given lifetime—that is, the number of them that our spirit Self and the Karmic Board decides we must deal with in this lifetime.

So how can you tell if you are in a Karmic Marriage? Well it is true to say that none of us really know what we could be getting into when we get married, this is because people grow and change, it is safe to say that the person you married at 19 years old will be a different person at 60, this is due to the fact that they have gone through Karma cycles through the years, and Karma is balanced, added to or paid back. So things we have not seen in people may surface later, or the very chemistry of the relationship brings out situations that one never suspected. So sometimes the bond is everlasting and sometimes it is a karmic marriage, so then you may ask how do we tell if a relationship we're in is keeping out our twin flame or if it's balancing karma? If there are a lot of problems, is it time for a divorce? Well, it may or may not be. I believe that you should work hard at any marriage. And we should try to make our marriages work. And if they don't work, we ought to be just as smart to recognize it and see to it that we don't overstay and create more karma and waste both partners' lives when we could actually be accomplishing more good without the burden of a relationship that is obviously leading neither party in any constructive direction.

Past Lives

We can all be described like Oceans, On the surface we can appear all fresh and clear brimming with life, but deep within us run the powerful undercurrents that make us who we are, these powerful undercurrents are of our souls memories, wants and needs, all borne of the effects of many incarnations on earth. They can cause us to love one person and yet despise another with intense ferocity, without really knowing why! They can cause us to feel fears or phobias which we can not understand, Patterns and habits will have formed deep within our inner consciousness which in turn shapes the way we will interact with people around us. It is extremely likely that almost everyone that are involved in some way in this, our present life, were also involved in our past lives also, and most likely that they have been involved in many, if not all of our past lives, Our Parents, siblings, children, friends even our bosses and work colleagues have all shared lives with us long before this present one, even our enemies were there, however all of these people were probably in different roles to the ones they are in now, and the effects they had on our souls in those past lives shape our experiences and the relationships that we share with them now, as the souls memories of all our past life experiences with others will serve to shape our innate reactions with them, and naturally, their souls past life memories of our past life interaction with them will shape and influence how they react to us now. Through the same eyes that the personality sees life, the soul sees it, but the soul looks with a memory covering centuries of passion and adventure, caring and love, hatred and revenge, doubt and fear. When we feel a seemingly unfounded fondness for another person, it is very likely due to soul memory of the positive role he or she played in our past lives. On the other hand, when we react with what seems to be an unfounded revulsion or hatred towards another person, you can be pretty sure it is because the soul recalls their past actions against us or our loved ones.

However, it is fair to say that the influences of past-life actions are rarely so clear cut. Often those who we have had many good lives and relationships with are probably the same people with who we have had many problems and disagreements, a mix of "good" and "bad karma," Actually it is quite uncommon that a past life relationship will have every aspect of life in good and clear focus, as Those positive, well-developed aspects from our past lives will give us much pleasure and support in the present. Equally, those aspects which we did not have in proper focus will give us opportunities for pain and growth in present relationships. Avoiding these influences is not possible. Whether we like it or not, the Law of Karma constantly brings before each of us the meeting of our past use of free will and consciousness. And so, what we have done to other souls as well as what they have done to us is reflected in the circumstances surrounding our present relationships and the basic, innate urges, attitudes and emotions we feel toward each other.

Soul Groups

The Ideas of past life relationships and how they influence our present life are not exclusive to individual relationships with people, they are also true of group relationships, from the very beginning of time our souls seemed to prefer to travel in groups, and the very act of travelling together for such long periods of time, created in us the attachment and need to build upon and maintain these group relationships , almost every soul on earth today were together in past ages in history, each group have shared the same times, such as the group here on earth now experiencing these modern times, were for instance the same group that shared, say, the ancient Egypt era, or maybe stone age times,

The souls who came in to this planetary system and entered the realms of consciousness associated with this region of the cosmos comprise our largest soul group. This group is then divided into subgroups that we call "the generations," which contain souls who then move through the natural cycles of Earth life together, these "generation" groups can then be further divided into the various nations, cultures, races, religions, etc., that have been formed during ages of interaction together Within these groups are the subgroups of souls who share similar philosophies, ideas, purposes, aspirations and attitudes. From here the soul groups further divide into the many smaller groups of personal relationships: communities, families, businesses, teams, schools and so on.

Soul groups create an attachment and loyalty amongst their members by not simply their shared experiences but also through their memories of how life has treated them and what they have come to mutually want, need and desire out of it, which is why certain eras and times reflect similar purposes, such as for example, the 60's were a time of free expression, brought on by the collective purpose, want, need and desire of that group, this in turn managed to affect changes in history, But don't get me wrong, Soul groups are not rigid nor static, and individual soul can use free will to seek an experience within another group, or indeed solo experiences within another group, there are many cases of souls changing allegiance, race or religion from one lifetime to another. Generation groups can also change, for example, two members of a family group who were mother and daughter in one life may change positions and become related in some other way in another life, they may even choose to be in the same generation in an incarnation as brothers, for example. However, they may choose not to be in the same family again. Although it is true to say that although soul groups are well established and will have a significant pull on the individuals within them, they do not have greater influence than an individual soul's will to change. Generally, however, soul groups will journey in and out of lives on earth together and during the same era,

To help explain some example of soul group incarnations, below I list the incarnations of two major soul groups

Soul Group 1: Early Atlantis - Early Ancient Egypt - Persia (during the time of Croseus I, II) - Palestine (during the time of Christ) - The Crusades - Colonial America

Soul Group 2: Late Atlantis- Late Ancient Egypt - Early Greece - Rome (during the time of Christ) - France (during the time of Louis XIV, XV, XVI) The American Civil War

Of course, these are only the most significant incarnations for these souls; they would most probably have incarnated many more times than the list indicates.

We should however explain that their would have been exceptions to these patterns as far as individual souls are concerned, as some souls do not always incarnate with their group, they may have chosen to go with a different group, or even to just 'sit that particular incarnation out' though they usually rejoined their original group eventually. Others decide to stay in spirit form and help those of us here on earth as maybe a guide, where they could help someone from their family group, or maybe a friend, but someone who they were connected with, so you see you do not actually have to incarnate in a flesh and blood form in each era that your group incarnates within, you can still be part of that era, and part of the family group, but in spirit form instead. While they live and work in that era you can help guide and teach them.

You will also find that a group of souls may find themselves together again even though not one single one of them actually wanted it to be that way. In these cases, it is often the forces of the Universal Law that have caused them to come together. For better or for worse they now have to meet the effects of their past actions with each other. The Universal intention is that the confrontation will lead to a resolution of their karma or at least recognition of how their past actions with each other have caused the present predicament, and they will resolve not to act that way again.

Be it individual or group relationships, the karmic effects of your past actions with others can and will create some very difficult, and in some cases even terrible situations. The meeting can result in atrocities such as murder, rape, torture and other equally nasty things. In not so serious cases karmic effect can result in bad feeling, back-stabbing, arguments, fighting amongst other things. Can you imagine what it would be like if Karmic law brought together a murder victim with their murderer? Or maybe two people who had suffered a betrayal, imagine what their reaction to each other would be in their new life? When lives are heavily weighed down by the negative effects of their past actions, their experience in the new life may be tragic. It can seem as if their life has been wasted, but look at it from the soul's point of view, it has not been wasted, a karmic lesson has been learned, and karma has been put into balance. And the next life incarnation will be a fuller one. Even though our 70 odd years in this life may seem short and final it is, in fact only a temporary visit, a visit to learn, to improve, to balance karma before the next visit

Parents and children

As hard as it may be for you to believe, each soul actually chooses its parents, the only exception to this rule is if a soul has abused its gift of free will, if this is the case then it comes then under the strong forces or universal law, or Karma, then it will be placed in a situation, (or family) where it will have to live through events where it will have to face up to the things it has done previously, these situations maybe extremely difficult , but it is important to bear in mind that no soul is given more than it can deal with, but I have to add at this point that that does not mean that everyone, that has had a terrible upbringing had been bad in a previous life, sometimes souls just pick families where situations will happen, in order to test themselves, others are just unlucky as the families they picked have used their free will to abuse others, but rest assured they WILL be made to pay through Karma next time, that saying 'what goes around comes around' is most defiantly true. It goes without saying that for those souls that have gone through lifetimes together and who have shared many experiences will be drawn together in a firmer way, be it good or bad, than they would with a soul who they have not had any past life experiences with, or indeed very little past life experiences, and so souls will pick the parents with whom they know will either teach them or allow them to encounter life experiences that they need to enable their soul to evolve , remember that when choosing the parents a soul will see the bigger picture, not just the childhood, they will get a general picture of what life will be like with that particular choice of parents in all its vastness with all its twists and turns, however the incoming soul can only really see the strongest pull in the would be parents lives and so It can't be sure that one of the free-willed parents won't change its mind and begin pursuing a different course, or that the twists and turns themselves won't change course and thereby change the family's future. It can't even be certain that it won't change its own mind once it joins that family.

Destiny and fate do indeed exist, and they exist side by side with free will. The effects of our past actions do as mentioned before have a resounding effect on our current lives, which helps to create our destiny. However, nothing surpasses the power of the soul's divinely-given free will. At any time we can use our will to change directions, change attitudes, change purposes, and change anything! In this way, our lives are both fatalistically foreshadowed by the cause-and effect forces of our past use of free will, and yet amenable to change by our present use of free will. Therefore, the incoming soul can see only the general course of the family's life path; it can't be sure the family will stay the course.

However it is not just up to the incoming soul as to which parents it chooses, it is fair to say the parents who are already here on earth also have a say as to what soul will go through life with them, as everything they do, think, desire and their purpose in life acts almost like a telephone up to the souls waiting to be reborn, this energy is responded to and a match will be made. This is particularly true of the mother. Although as I am sure you would expect, more than one incoming soul may be drawn to the same mother-to-be. In these cases, the forces of cause and effect, the will power and desire of the mother and the souls wanting to incarnate combine to make the selection. The souls who were not chosen for the present entry may well come in through a later pregnancy if the opportunity is presented. Thereby becoming siblings of the souls who entered first; or they may go on to other families with whom friendships or other blood relationships would naturally form and be maintained with the original channel family. The soul generally enters the baby body at or near the time of birth.

Chapter 5
Soul Mates & Twin Flames

What are Twin Flames

The quest for love and for that perfect mate is really a quest for wholeness, and there are three types of romantic relationships that help lead one to this wholeness: twin flames, soul mates and karmic relationships. Now I am often, in my work asked, so what is the difference? How will I know who is who? And does it matter? Well yes, it matters, in the previous chapter I spoke about Karmic relationships and karmic marriages, and I will attempt to answer for you the rest of the questions outlined above in this chapter, but in order not to make things to complicated it is best, I feel to split the sub chapters in order to answer bit by bit, and then hopefully, the plan is, that by the time you have completed chapter 5 you will have a broad understanding of all three types of relationships.

So off we go, firstly Twin Flames –

the term twin flame is not to be confused with soul mates, as these two are distinctly different, the story of Twin flames is the greatest love story ever told, Twin flames were created together in the beginning and share a unique destiny. Created in a single fiery ovoid, they were separated into two spheres of being—one in a masculine polarity and the other in a feminine polarity—but each with the same pattern of divine identity. Though they spend some lifetimes together and others apart, their tie is eternal, and after they have each united with their Higher Self they will be together forever. But not all the beautiful and soul fulfilling loves are those of twin flames. The story goes that **A**eons ago beyond the confines of time and space, you and your twin flame stood before the mother and father gods Alpha and Omega,, and you vowed to take with you to earth a portion of God's creativity to bring energy from the Spirit plane, into the world of physical form for action, for good works and then to return to the spirit plane after having mastered time and space. However learning to translate spiritual energy to the physical plane required a series of incarnations (lifetimes) in both masculine and feminine embodiments. In this way, each twin flame had the opportunity to reflect the fullness of the Father as well as the Mother God. Had we remained in constant harmony, we would have shared the beauty of the relationship of cosmic lovers throughout our many incarnations on earth. But as soon as we lost our harmony with each other and with God through mistrust, through fear, or through a sense of separation from our divine identity we allowed darkness to enter our lives, creating worlds of negative energy between us and our twin flame. We found ourselves further and further apart until we simply passed as ships in the night, tragically unaware of each other's existence.

Each incarnation apart from our twin flame was spent either creating negative karma or balancing some of the karma that stood in the way of our reunion. At times we assumed various relationships with our twin flame husband/wife, mother/son, father/daughter, and sister/brother in order to unwind the negative strands of energy we had woven into our subconscious through our misuse of free will.

Often, when people learn that they share a unique mission with their twin flame, they begin to search physically for that one special soul instead of seeking their wholeness within. So you can rest assured that somewhere in cosmos, each one of us has our very own divine other, who carries either the feminine or masculine polarity. This soul memory of the twin flame is so powerful, that we can feel very alone in this world, as we search for that promise of that original perfect love, the twin. No other love can compare to your own twin flame. They are quite literary, your other half, the other half or you, your twin flame! So who can they be? How can we find them? well the finding the part comes later in this chapter, but as for who they can be, generally, the twin flame relationship is found among spouses, friends, occasionally as parent and child, however sometimes the twin flame isn't even incarnate at the same time. However, there does seem to be a pattern that most twin flame relationships follow. In their early incarnations together they tend to be mates or at least seek a lover's relationship with each other, while in later incarnations with each other they tend to seek less sexually involved relationships and more work-related activities together, especially when the work has a soul purpose. This could be due to the involution/evolution process where, in the early periods of the descent into materiality they tended to continue their self-seeking, self-satisfying pursuits; but on the ascent toward a return to spirituality they tended to seek more holistic purposes and relationships. That is not to say that all present sexual relationships are self-seeking

The separation of twin flames

As said before, the twin flames are split originally and each half are supposed to learn their life lessons, however the two halves sometimes cross paths during various lifetimes, they have a cosmic powerful bond because they really are of the same soul. They complete each other. They are often very much alike, and the intensity of the connection is extremely intense, and it is fair to say that unless you are at the correct time in your life as far as development in life lessons it may seem too much for a mere human with emotions and issues to handle, so you painfully end up parting ways. When you both finish your lessons, you are both reunited in heaven and come together as a beautiful representation of love and unity. However if you meet at the right time, an amazing love and bond comes into action and you will both feel so total, so complete, the perfect relationship, but do not think that because of this then you will never have any problems, as this is not the case, because of the intense feelings and emotions, situations can get heated and difficult, this is why unless you are ready for this relationship it will not work, but if you work through things then I can tell you, there will never be anything better!

How do you recognise your twin flame?

I am often asked at this point, does this twin flame person really exist? Of course they exist. And clearly if you needed to ask that, then you have not yet been lucky enough to have been rejoined by yours, as you will know when you meet them, you will simply just know when it happens to you. The thing with twin flames is that it is spiritual. This person has a profound effect on you. It's a feeling like this person should be in your life. They can inflict great pain or great joy in you. The joy comes from being able to share a relationship with them. The pain comes from being apart from them or when they choose to not reciprocate your feelings... When you meet up with your twin flame, you'll be really attracted to that person and drawn to them magnetically. Your feelings for them will naturally grow stronger and very intense. You will feel as if you just "know them totally" even when you have just meet them, you will simply slot into place next to them and when you realize you have met a your twin flame, it can be a traumatic experience. This person will have such a profound effect on you that you can't shake off. Even being apart or separated from them can cause emptiness in your soul.

So is there anything that you can do to assist you in finding your twin flame? And if you are going through life, am I saying that you should not partake in other relationships? No of course I am not, as not everyone will meet with their twin flame in this life time, and other relationships will help with karma as well as life lessons so they are necessary, but what I am saying is that there is a difference in how each of these relationships feel, also I think that it is your individual free will, your personal decision. If you are intent on pursuing the Path of your life and more permanent things, you have to realize that the establishment of such relationships takes time and energy and a certain amount of input because every friendship demands the giving of self. And so you've only got energy and time and space to spend in this embodiment—it's like a bank account. Every individual has to decide what he wants to do with his life and life-force. But I always think, if you're locked into a wrong relationship or you've settled for less, you could miss your twin flame. One of the reasons we are separated from our twin flames is because the Law compels us to manifest our own interior wholeness first. Wholeness is a magnet, and it magnetizes to our wholeness. So if we are incomplete in consciousness or if we harbour within ourselves records of grief or fear or death or dying or problems of no forgiveness of our twin flame from past lives, this is inside of us and it's a block to finding the perfect match. So we can spend a lot of time going from relationship to relationship and actually never arriving at that union.

So what if you find it difficult to recognise your twin flame? Well although that can happen, generally you will just know, it is the intense draw and attraction that kinda gives it away , but if you want to be sure, you can connect in with your angels, and ask them to show you your twin flame, and help to bring them to you. That's what I did ! I got disheartened constantly looking and not finding, so I asked Archangel Michael to bring him to me, and sure enough he did, it was clearly helped by the fact that I was ready to meet him and he with me, but it was amazing when I did ! it was not so much fire works, more a feeling that I was now complete, it felt right and normal, and I was sure I had met him somewhere before, of course I now know that I had, but it was not in this life,

I do understand though that there are a lot of you out there desperate for more guidelines to help in their search, as it can be difficult at times to be able to tell the difference between your twin flame and someone who is very similar, for example , you could be in a relationship with someone who seems almost perfect for you, but also has one or two undesirable characteristics, would this mean that they are not right for you? Well it is wise to remember that most people have a collection of good and bad qualities. And basically we do decide on our regular relationships based on what we can live with in a person given the fact that there's a greater love that binds us. That saying, "love is blind" or "love will conquer all " springs to mind at this point, but determining who your twin flame is by a person's good and bad qualities is not always such a safe method because the knowledge of the twin flame is very inner. And personal as mentioned above. And so it's almost best to blind yourself to that persons characteristics to a certain extent and really listen to your inner self and to follow the flame of the heart. Sometimes outer examination and analysis can be very misleading. So if you feel you are in this kind of relationship, and you are sure that it is not say a "karmic Relationship" then go ahead and ask Archangel Michael to confirm for you if this is your Twin Flame or not. But remember to listen carefully, because he will answer you if you give him the opportunity to. But if you don't want to know because you want this person more than you want the Truth, then you can get into trouble. Some have said that they knew he / she was the "one" their Twin Flame, by how "he perfectly mirrored the aspects inside of me" meaning that they mirrored all your aspects and emotions that make up who you are including all the ones that you keep well hidden deep inside you like all your anger and yin self). I believe that you can also recognise your twin flame by how they look, almost as if they are how you feel your inner masculine self would look, or inner female self would look if you are male, that not to say that they look like you how you are now, but how you feel you would be if you were the opposite sex, in the way of temperament, build, shape and so on. They can also appear to be the opposite of you in looks like having the opposite of everything like dark hair when you have very blond hair, bright blue eyes that take up everything while your pupils take up everything; very plump lips when you have them very thin stuff like that. You can also recognise him/ her by looking into their eyes, their inner soul, if this makes you feel comfortable, or maybe in awe, or relaxed; they could be the "one"

Contact of Twin Flames

Your twin flame may have already won this soul liberation and have been reunited with the higher beings or he may still be struggling to find the way. Where your twin flame is and what his state of consciousness is can greatly influence your own ability to find them and in turn find fulfilment and wholeness. Because both of you share the same blueprint of identity totally unique to the two of you whatever energy you send forward is imprinted or stamped with that specific pattern. According to the law of like attracts like, all energy you release makes it way to your twin flame which can either hinder or help him on the path to fulfilment and wholeness which in turn could result in you both finding each other. When you send forward love or hope, these qualities will uplift your twin flame. But if you are burdened with frustration or hatred, your twin flame will also feel the weight of these feelings. Sometimes the inexplicable joys or depressions you feel are the moods of your other half registering on your own consciousness.

Now there are ways which has been shown to work really well that can push forward your progress to making contact with your Twin Flame, one way that I used to use was to meditate and to make the following invocation

> *"In the name of Christ I call to the blessed I AM Presence of our twin flames for the sealing of our hearts as one for the victory of our mission to humanity. I invoke the light of the Holy Spirit for the consuming of all negative karma limiting the full expression of our divine identity and the fulfilment of our divine plan."*

By doing this, it will not matter if you are living in different spheres you can unite spiritually on higher planes and direct light into your own world and the world of your twin flame for the balancing of mutual karma. This inner contact magnifies the light and attainment you each have and releases the awesome amazing power of the polarity of your love, enabling you to stand strong against the conflicts that inevitably come to the door of all who would defend love.

What is a Soul Mate ?

As mentioned in the Twin Flame chapter a soul mate connection is very different from that of the twin flame. Whereas we each have only one twin flame, we can have many soul mates. not many people are lucky enough to have rejoined with their twin flames, and but many more of us if not all of us have met soul mates, and it is comforting to know that There is also the love of close, kindred souls which are our soul mates. Soul mates as said earlier are different from twin flames, in that they were not created from the same ovoid of light and therefore each has their own twin flame. The soul mate relationship is a great blessing when for some reason we cannot reunite with our twin flame in this embodiment. For instance, our twin flame might not be in embodiment at this time, or may not be following a spiritual path, or conversely, May already be an Ascended Master working in the spiritual realms to inspire us upward. An ascended twin flame might even send a soul mate to us as a representative of him/herself. Soul mates are drawn together because they are simultaneously working on the same type of karma, sacred labour and the same chakra. Soul mates share a complementary calling in life. They can be partners, friends, family and workmates and can be the same or the opposite sex who are often working to develop the same virtues and to master the same chakras. These relationships tend to be harmonious and satisfying, and such kindred souls can accomplish great things together. They can become some of the most powerful friendships you will ever have. And many of these soul mate relationships can end in romantic relationships and marriages which can be wonderful pairings, it can appear at times to be difficult to tell that they are not twin flames, however, if you have already met with your twin flame earlier on in life, but it was the wrong time and you parted you will find that you describe the twin flame relationship as "the love of your life" albeit in private ! and it will seem that although you love the soul mate relationship that you find yourself in, there is always a secret(or in some cases not so secret) longing for the other person, if this is you then it is not difficult for you to tell the difference, but for those of you that have not met up with your twin flame, a soul mate relationship or marriage can seem wonderful and perfect for you, and please do not see it as putting up with second best, because it is not, as said earlier not many of us are lucky enough to have met up with our twin flames, and so a soul mate marriage will be amazingly strong and good. But although you may be forgiven for assuming that a marriage between two soul mates should also be able to handle challenging times as well as the great times, but that may not always be the case. Just because they are in tune to one another, are each willing to take responsibility for their role in contributing to the conflict, and are both committed to making the marriage a successful one the marriage can still fall apart if other essentials such as love, respect, and communication are missing. Many people are now married to a soul mate, but it would be wise to realise that just because they are your soul mate, or maybe even your twin flame, do not fall into complacency, so many people make the mistake of taking these relationships for granted, even if they are a soul mate or twin flame , you still need to work at it, especially if it is a twin flame relationship as they are also the ones that can hurt you the most! Because of the deep love you feel. So do not take your relationship for granted. If you start looking for perfection in your spouse, or think that everything in your relationship should immediately click, and that there won't be any problems, you are setting yourself up for a dose of heavy disillusionment. There can also be temptation to bail out of an unhappy marriage because you think your spouse can't be your soul mate because you're unhappy but please bear in mind that if you think that marrying your soul mate will mean a life free from hard times and conflict, you are not facing reality. However If you really believe that your spouse is not your soul mate don't just walk away from the relationship for that reason alone. Spend some time getting to know yourself a bit better first. You can't find your soul mate if you haven't found yourself. You should remember that not all of the beautiful and soul-fulfilling loves are those of twin flames. Soul mates experience a calmer, more stable connection which can be on the lines of a brother and a sister type rapport. And some times the very best marriages are between soul mates as they work very harmoniously together in business, raising children, and contributing to the community.

How do you recognise your Soul Mate?

In order to recognize your soul mate, you must first know yourself. Once that is done my list below should also help you to recognise your soul mate, this list is not exclusive and is a guide for you only

Soul mate marriages can be well balanced, strong, and positive. There should be a lack of intimidation, manipulation, or abuse in a marriage of soul mates. A soul mate should make you feel safe.

A relationship with a soul mate is a natural fit and usually feels like it is meant to be. Even so, every marriage, even a marriage of soul mates, takes the two spouses giving priority to their marriage relationship. A marriage to a soul mate is filled with honesty and support. But then, so are successful marriages of couples who don't believe they are soul mates. There is a sense of familiarity and mutuality in a marriage to a soul mate as well as in long lasting marriages. Soul mate marriages can be healthy, passionate and harmonious. Soul mate partners can easily get a lot done by working together. Couples who are soul mates often take joy in watching the growth of one another. A soul mate will accept who you are, will bring out the best in you, challenge you, and are your best friend. A soul mate will not require you to change. Soul mates relish small moments together and cherish their commitment to their marriage

Bearing all the above in mind it is important to be wary of looking for a mate who is ideal and who feels and thinks exactly the way you do. No one can live up to that kind of standard. Soul mates don't agree on everything. And don't use the soul mate concept as an excuse to walk away from your commitment to your marriage. Remember you can still have difficult times even when married to your soul mate. Romance is a gamble. Marriage takes attentiveness. And the Bottom line that is marrying a soul mate isn't necessary in order to have a successful and happy marriage.

Chapter 6
Exercises

Protecting Yourself

Psychic protection is in my opinion one of the most overlooked subjects as well as one of the most overlooked, however it is also one of the most needed subjects to be learned. There are many different ways of using psychic protection, and you will find that most psychics will have their own personal favourite method, I will endeavour to show you a few of my favourites in this chapter but if you feel like altering them slightly to suit you then please do so, as if they "fit" with you then they will work better with you also. But first I had better explain to you why you need protection.

Linking to Spirit has got its very positive side but if we are not trained correctly we will soon find the negative energies. This can lead to a psychic attack and you might experience unwelcome psychic and spiritual communication and attention. Now in our homes, we have doors, locks, windows, burglar alarms, even panic buttons all to protect us, and we always use them, but they protect against living people, the spirit world and the people of the spirit world are of a different construct and vibration, for Inhabitants of this plane, there are no doors, locks or windows to stop them, a ghost can walk into your house and sit next to you as can a lower form, thankfully it doesn't happen too often, but at some time it may happen to you or a member of your family. We are under threat as we cannot see these spirits, most of the time we are totally unaware they are even there unless you are sensitive or clairvoyant, you may ask why they would attack me. Sadly lower forms are no different than some people in this world who will attack you in the street for no reason, others it's how they are its fun to them. The difference is you can see them and have some comeback if the police and justice system do their job correctly. These spirits can be crafty not only that you can't see them, Trust me just because you can't see them does not mean they don't exist no more than you can't see TV pictures in your home without a TV.

If you are purposely opening up to work with the spirit world then again protection is also needed, now the methods are the same for either reason, you can use a variety of methods, but I always make sure that all my chakra points are closed once I have finished with my work with the spirit world, and if I feel under threat at anytime I will again always check that I am closed down and if necessary I will carry out a closing visualisation to restore peace. It can never harm you to close yourself down even when you thought you were already closed and it can help you to close down if you have inadvertently 'opened up'. This is what I will do –

Closing down

Always be respectful and courteous when directing any thoughts or words to Spirit which can be hard when you are frightened. But remember to Thank Spirit for all they have shown and imparted during your communication. Ask Spirit to withdraw their energies and thank them for choosing to communicate.
Breathe deeply, focus, and imagine closing and bolting a secure door on each of the chakra points which are as follows
The crown chakra – on the top of your head
The third eye which is just above the bridge of your nose, above your eyebrows in the middle
The throat chakra
The heart chakra
The solar plexus

The sacral
After closing the heavy door, draw a heavy curtain across the door
Now visualise yourself, your loved ones and your home or place that you are in sealed in a ring of white light. Picture this ring of light going around your home or the place you are at.
Do this whenever you feel the need, the more you do this the stronger you get,
The other way I use is after closing my chakras I visualise getting into a shower, but instead of water coming down to wash me, it is the golden ray of Christ,
If you go through the same exercises each time you open up and close down it will strengthen your ability to switch on and off. Make it unique and special to you and make it part of your everyday spiritual practice and routine. It is the best self-defence you can give yourself.

Protection from negative Spirit

If you work with the Spirit world, protection is the name of the game first. We must learn to trust our helpers or guides to protect us from all negative Spirit but you need to ask them to. Once you ask your helpers to protect then they will do after all they asked us to be their communication vessel for them (medium) so it is only right that we can ask them to protect us, I do believe in the Lords Prayer that it is a special message of Protection.. As we work with Spirit we will go to visiting places which may have a presence, unknown or known... it is best to protect again using the Power of the Prayer... When for any reason we meet a negative soul, firmly tell the spirit being to step back, also at the same time placing your self in an egg-shape oval filled with the brightest light. White or blue and ask spirit helpers to make the eggshell to be so hard that all negative spirit bounds of this egg. Hoping that they will be bounced back to where they come from

A Walk with your Angel

A Walk with Your angel
   Here is one guided visualization that is often effective and is found in many variations (you may want to tape this so that you can close your eyes while doing the visualization)

Allow your self to Relax, relax completely...
Imagine yourself walking in a beautiful garden on the edge of a forest...
The garden is full of wild flowers, ... birds fly above you
Singing sweetly... the Sun shines brightly...
Walk on among the beautiful flowers continue walking across the meadow toward the trees..
Now from the trees you become aware of your Angel approaching you...
You walk toward your angel who moves forward, to meet you.
Open your heart as your angel meets and embraces you.
Feel the love and understanding of your own angel, who has known you always and loves you unconditionally...
Walk with your angel in the beautiful garden listen and hear,
See, feel the message of your angels LOVE and continued presence in your life.
Walk with your angel and receive the gift of understanding from your angel
Tell your angel what simple sign you will look for to sense guidance in your daily life
perhaps red green and yellow lights, or left ear tickle for yes right ear for no and nose for unclear
know that questions with yes and no answers can be misunderstood fairly easily and you will need to practice neutrality to get the clearest answers from your angel.
Your angel sees all possibilities and while they are rarely wrong they and your reception of guidance can be affected by your desire for a particular outcome and the future is not an absolute it is influenced by free will.
Now as time comes to return to yourself embrace your angel

And slowly gently return to your self in the now
Knowing that you can always return to the garden and your angel and
Your angel will be learning to communicate with you as you learn to be aware of them.

Ascension and healing

Ascension and Healing to facilitate spiritual expansion.

This kind of meditation should be done very often at least once a week, if you want to ascend. Doing meditations like this often accelerates your path greatly and makes feel better, because of the cleansing from negative energies and removing of emotional dirt. Ask Archangel Michael to protect you.

Relax with some gentle music and maybe light some candles, Ask your guides to protect you..
Ask Archangel Raphael to heal and enlighten your grounding cord to the centre of the earth. You can also ask the centre of the earth itself to help you. "Centre of the earth, help me" Mantra: "I am connected to the centre of the earth" Ask Archangel Gabriel to help you.
Ask Archangel Gabriel to cleanse, heal and open your root chakras.
Ask Archangel Gabriel to cleanse, heal and open your sacral chakras. Ask archangel Uriel to help you.
Ask archangel Uriel to cleanse, heal and open the solar plexus. Ask archangel Chamuel to help you.
Ask archangel Chamuel to cleanse, heal and open all your heart chakras. Ask Archangel Michael to help you.
Ask Archangel Michael to cleanse, heal and open throat chakra. Ask Archangel Raphael to help you.
Ask Archangel Raphael to cleanse, heal and open the forehead chakra.
Ask Archangel Raphael to cleanse, heal and open the third eye.
Ask Archangel Raphael to cleanse, heal and open the earth star. Ask archangel Jophiel to help you.

Angelic Karma

Ask archangel Jophiel to cleanse, heal and open you crown chakras.
Ask archangel Zadkiel to help.
Ask archangel Zadkiel to cleanse, heal and open the 8:Th main centre 7cm above your head.
Ask archangel Zadkiel to cleanse, heal and open the soul star. Ask pure light from the Holy Christ.
Ask pure light from your own monad. Ask Holy Christ to enlighten all your bodies.
Ask archangel Metatron to increase your light level. Ask Archangel Michael to cut all negative cords. Ask your monad and archangel Raphael to heal you.
Ask your monad and archangel Raphael to heal your physical body. Ask your monad and ascended masters to raise your vibrational level to highest level. Ask healing energy from archangels, ascended masters, Holy Christ
and from your monad. Ask Mahatma Energy to help you and come to your body.
It will come to your body if you ask it to come.
The mahatma energy is very high vibrational and
it rises your vibrational level. The energies are more useful to you, if you remember
that you have to stay grounded to be able to use
the higher spiritual energies in here and get
the negative energies go to the centre of the earth
automatically. Mantra: "Negative energies go to the centre of the earth" Ask archangels to anchor your 4 dimensional chakras.
"Archangel Gabriel, anchor my 4th dimensional root chakra"
"Archangel Gabriel, anchor my 4th dimensional sacral chakra"
"Archangel Uriel, anchor my 4th dimensional solar plexus"
"Archangel Chamuel, anchor my 4th dimensional heart chakras"
"Archangel Michael, anchor my 4th dimensional throat chakras"
"Archangel Raphael, anchor my 4th dimensional third eye"
"Archangel Raphael, anchor my 4th dimensional forehead chakra"
"Archangel Jophiel, anchor my 4th dimensional crown chakra" You can anchor 5th-9th dimensional chakras same way, but
don't anchor 5th and 6th dimensional chakras until you have cleansed your energies and 3rd dimensional chakras and have some sort of

mastery of them. Don't anchor 7th-9th dimensional chakras before you have passed at least 5th main initiation (monadic merger). Ask your monad to anchor to you. You monad is your God self, what is same thing as Mighty I Am Presence or thought adjuster mentioned in the Urantia book. Before you have fustigated with your monad, you can channel the monad, by asking it to connect to you and anchor to you. Ask your monad to cleanse you from negative emotions. Ask your monad to remove all fears and negativeness from you. Ask you monad to remove all bad and negative thoughts from you. Ask purification of the violet flame from archangel Zadkiel or from St. Germain. If you have negative beings in your field, ask Archangel Michael to remove astral entities from you.Ask Archangel Michael to take bad or lost spirits where they belong. Thank archangels and masters for help.
Do this meditation often!

Cleansing the Aura

CLEANSING THE AURA

THE CLEANSING VORTEX

This exercise is a visualization exercise for cleansing and purifying your entire auric field. It is an excellent exercise to perform at the end of a day, especially at those times when you have interacted with a great many people. It helps sweep out energy debris, preventing it from accumulating and creating imbalance within the auric field. It only takes about five minutes to be effective.

1. Take a seated position and perform a progressive relaxation. Performing the breathing technique just described is beneficial as a preparation for this exercise. You may want to use a simple prayer or mantra as well. Remember that the exercise as presented here is a guideline, and you should learn to adapt it to your own energies

2. About 20 feet above you, in your mind's eye, visualize a small whirlwind of crystalline white fire beginning to form. It looks like a small, visualize it so that it is large enough to encompass your entire auric field. The small end of the funnel should be visualized as capable of entering through the crown of your head and passing down the middle pillar of your body .

3. This whirlwind of spiritual fire should be seen as rotating and spinning clockwise. As it touches your aura, see it as sucking up and burning off all of the energy debris you have accumulated.

4. See, fell and imagine it moving down, over and through your entire aura and body. Know that it is sweeping your energy field clean of all the extraneous energies you have accumulated throughout the day.

5. As it moves through your body, allow this energy vortex to exit out through your feet down into the heart of the earth itself. See the vortex as carrying this energy debris into the lower realms, where it is used to fertilize and benefit the lower kingdoms of life upon and within the planet.

Dolphin Meditation

Find a nice peaceful place, maybe even lie on your bed, make sure you are warm enough, and the phones and all things that could disturb you are switched off

If you can play some relaxing music, even maybe light a candle or some incense, take a few nice deep breaths, letting the stressed of the day flow away out of you.

Check you have a bubble of white light around your self, if you have not imagine placing your self into one, so that you are protected, anything you feel safe in, that can open and close.

Now as you breathe in and out, in and out, let your body start to really relax, start to hear the ebbing and flowing of the see, maybe breath with each ebb and flow, feel as if you are becoming at one with the sea. As you continue to breathe now more gently, more now slowly, I want you to feel the sand beneath your feet, and the sun is shining, you are feeling so safe, so warm and relaxed.

As you walk along by the seas edge you notice that the sea is calm, and feels like the water is calling to you. But as you look out to the sea, you can see something moving in the water coming towards you. You do not feel in danger as you know they are a friend. As your friend gets closer you realize that your friend is a dolphin, come to take you on a journey of self discovery, your dolphin is there to protect you and guide you.

As the dolphin swims right up to the land nearly, you climb on the dolphins back, and as you swim to wards the open sea with your dolphin and his dolphin friends, you start to feel free of all life, all stresses, you are free.

The dolphin is going to take you to all different places within the sea, to hidden caves, hidden cities, to meet mermaids, where ever it is, go be free. Feel your journey.

It does not matter if you fall asleep, if that is what you need. It does not matter if your dolphin takes you back to shore. Just go on your journey and when you are ready, find your way back to the shore, feel the sand again, then feel where you are in your bed, chair, on your floor, and take a few breaths again to totally be back fully.

Write down your experiences, a meditation diary is always good to look back on, as meditations can give answers some times.

Meet your Spirit Guide visualisation
Meet your spirit guides

Meditation is not hard to master, despite all those books on the technique that make it appear so! It's simply a wonderful and beneficial relaxation technique.

Here is a very basic meditation to meet your Lifetime Guide.

Relax as best you can. Undoubtedly, you will have numerous thoughts of your day's events, etc, flow into your mind, this is very normal. Don't concern yourself with them, simply acknowledge them, and then let them go.

Please ensure that you read up on the grounding and shielding exercises and apply them first as always!!!!

Meditation

Find a comfortable chair and sit down. Ensure you will not be disturbed for 15mins and switch your mobile off!

Close your eyes, feet flat on the floor and relax. Take several deep breaths and start the grounding exercise.

Once you have done this, follow with the shielding exercise and relax in your pure, white loving bubble.

Take several more deep breaths as breath helps to link us with spirit, and relax every muscle in your body. Take your time doing this and work down from your face to your feet.

Once you are fully relaxed, say either aloud or mentally; 'my dearest Spirit Guide, I welcome you to join me now. Please touch me to confirm you are with me now.'

It's important to remain fully relaxed and have no expectations. Just see what may occur. Ask again and wait.

Dismiss nothing, no matter how slight or trivial!

You may experience; Cold/warm air; a tickle on any part of your body; sensation of walking through a cobweb, sensation of a fly on your face; goose bumps; feeling of someone touching your hair, head, neck or shoulders; suddenly feeling tearful, emotional, overwhelming joy, love or excitement.

If you experience anything like this, trust it!

Ask for your guide to touch you three times to confirm their presence.

Don't worry if you 'feel' nothing, try again later.

Once you have made contact with your guide, you can take it slowly each day, and start to ask questions like what is your name, and so forth.

Always give thanks when you are finished.

A Healing Meditation with Archangel Raphael

Healing Meditation with Archangel Raphael
You can work with Archangel Raphael and his healing energy using meditation.

To prepare say a prayer to Mother/Father/God/Arch Angel Raphael, to please help you be as open to the healing as possible and to join in the healing work and support you through your healing process.

Sit comfortably where you will not be disturbed. Begin by grounding and centering yourself. Close your eyes and imagining roots growing from your feet into Mother Earth. Then follow this simple breathing exercise to relax your physical body: breathe in through your nose, hold it for 7 seconds, and release it very slowly through your mouth. Repeat 3 times then unconsciously continue breathing this way throughout the meditation. Tell you're Ego-self to move toward your left shoulder. Let the Ego-self know that it's only an observer during the healing and know this is so. Ask God/dess to send down a beam of protective white light. God/dess hears your request and in your mind's eye you immediately envision a beam of light coming down from the universe. Watch it surround you in a protective glow.

Call Archangel Raphael, either mentally or out loud and ask. "Archangel Raphael please come to me now and assists me in my healing." If you like, also invite in your Higher Self and your own Spirit Guides and Guardian Angels. You don't need to know their names, just say "Spirit Guides and Guardian Angels, please join Archangel Raphael in my healing session."

In your mind's eye, picture Raphael standing over you with his hands outstretched over your head. See the healing energy in the form of green light flowing from his hands down into your body through your crown chakra (the top of your head). Try to relax and feel the energy. You may not be able to feel the energy at first, but after doing this a few times (if needed); you will probably begin to become more sensitive to the energy. Most people feel the healing energy as warmth or tingling. Others feel a soft and loving stream running through their body. Whatever you feel is right for you.

The first time, let this energy flow through you for a while, opening you to Archangel Raphael's curative energy and preparing you on all levels to accept the healing. This initial step can last for several minutes or until you feel that it is time to move on to the next step.

Now change the focus onto specific parts of your body. Picture Raphael's hands over these areas and feel and see the green light flowing through his hands to your injury or area of illness.

When you are through, thank Archangel Raphael, and ask him to protect you from negative thoughts and feelings that manifest into health problems. Also thank your Spirit Guides and Angels for assisting in the healing.

Focus on grounding and centering yourself. Again, picture the roots from your feet into Mother Earth.

Now open your eyes.

It does not matter if you are good at visualization, or whether or not you can physically feel the healing energy from Archangel Raphael and your intentions are what you are healed by. This method works with injuries and illnesses equally well.

You may repeat this work several times a day if necessary, or whenever you feel you need it.

Once you are used to healing work with Archangel Raphael, your Spirit Guides and Angels, you can ask them for quick relief and healing. This is especially helpful for chronic conditions they regularly work with you on such as pain relief.

Please remember to thank Archangel Raphael, your Guides and Angels for their help. It's not necessary but they really appreciate the acknowledgment that you know they are their working with you. You can also take the time and opportunity to talk with them, either telepathically in your mind or softly out loud. They do hear what you say and acknowledge in ways that they can, even if you can't hear their responses back to you in words.

Healing Others with Archangel Raphael's Energy

you can also work with Archangel Raphael to heal others. We are all beings of light and anyone can work with the healing energy and assist in another person's healing. You do not need any special training to do this type of healing work. You just act as a channel for the healing energy. All that is needed is your intention to help the other person in their highest good. Archangel Raphael, your Higher Self and Spirit Guides, and the Higher Self and Spirit Guides of the person you are doing the healing work with are directing the healing being done. Your main job is support for the person, or "receiver," and to facilitate the healing work.

Make the person you are going to work on comfortable by having them sit in a chair or lay down. Together, ask your ego-selves to move toward your left shoulders. Let the ego-selves know they are only observers during the healing and know this is so. Ask your Angels, Guides and the receiver's Angels and Guides to accompany you on this quest to heal now. Ask God/dess to send down a beam of protective white light. God/dess hears your request and in your mind's eye you can immediately envision a beam of light coming down from the universe. Watch it surround you and the receiver in a protective glow.

Both of you say, out loud, "Archangel Raphael please come to us now and assist in the healing in [Healer's highest good and that [Receiver] accepts the healing in their own highest good.

Of course, all of this can be done silently. The person being healed doesn't have to participate in the prayers and invitation. But it is helpful if they do take an active role in the healing.

Place your hands on or above the person's head. Picture Archangel Raphael standing behind you and working through you. Try to envision or feel the healing green light energy flowing from Archangel Raphael into your hands and then into the crown chakra of the receiver. Your hands may become warm from the energy.

After several minutes of this, move on to specific areas of the body where it is needed the most. Trust your own feelings and guidance on the length of time to spend on each area and where to place your hands.

You could be guided to work on areas that have nothing to do with the areas of the symptoms, disease or injury. This could be underlying causes or just a separate need for healing in that area of the body. Just follow your intuition.

When you are through, don't forget to thank Archangel

Raphael and the spirits involved.

Printed in the United Kingdom by
Lightning Source UK Ltd., Milton Keynes
140505UK00001B/43/P